WELLSPRINGS OF SCRIPTURE

WELLSPRINGS
of SCRIPTURE

by J. Massingberd Ford

University of Notre Dame

SHEED AND WARD: NEW YORK

This book is dedicated in appreciation to the Reverend Professor Noel Quinton King and to all my former colleagues in the Department of Religious Studies, Makerere University College, University of East Africa.

May the Shekinah ever overshadow them.

Contents

vii

Introduction

Then Israel sang this song:
"Spring up, O well!—Sing to it!—
the well which the princes dug,
which the nobles of the people delved,
with the scepter and with their staves" (Num. 21:17–18).

The well of water has been taken frequently as a symbol of the revelation of God, especially his revelation enshrined in holy scripture. In the Jewish documents discovered in 1947 the following interpretation of the Song of the Well occurs:

The Well is the Law, and those who dug it were the converts of Israel . . . God called them all *princes* because they sought Him, and their renown was disputed by no man. The *Stave* is the Interpreter of the Law of whom Isaiah said, *He makes a tool for His work* (Isa. 54:16); and the *nobles of the people* are those who come to dig the *Well* with the staves with which the *Stave* ordained that they should walk in all the age of wickedness . . . until he comes who shall teach righteousness at the end of days (*Damascus Rule*, VI).[1]

Those who are able to draw living water from the well of life gain life for themselves and give life to others. Jesus announced in John 7:37–39,

[1] G. Vermes, *The Dead Sea Scrolls in English* (Penguin Books, Baltimore, 1962), pp. 102–103, used with permission.

ix

"If any one thirst, let him come to me and drink. He who believes in me, as the scripture has said, 'Out of his heart shall flow rivers of living water.'" Now this he said about the Spirit. . . .

Water, which preserves physical life, is a potent symbol of the Holy Spirit, who gives spiritual life. It is from the pages of scripture that one imbibes the Holy Spirit, who regenerates the soul.

This book is designed to be like the scattered wells which refreshed the patriarchs as they wandered over the desert and to give a taste of living water to the reader. Only certain themes of scripture have been selected, but it is hoped that these will lead the reader to "join rope to rope and delve deeper."

A word of explanation is needed for the teachers and students who adopt this book as a text for classroom study.

The writer, both as a student and as a teacher, has attended various schools of theology in Britain, America, and Africa. On the whole, she found that two approaches to the study of sacred scripture for the nonspecialist prevailed in those schools. One approach comprised a survey course, which covered most of the bible, so that the students were given an introduction to each book. In this type of course much time was devoted to discussion of the date, authorship, composition, and historical accuracy of individual parts of the bible. The average student tended to lose himself in such details and failed to comprehend both the unity of the two Testaments and their related theology. The other approach was to select two to four biblical books and study them in depth. This usually proved the better plan, but it meant that much of the bible was left untouched.

The present book has attempted to find a balance between the two approaches. Certain sections of the bible have been

selected to represent (1) the different types of biblical literary genre—historical, prophetic, sapiential—and (2) the
major events of salvation history. The developing theme of
the covenant love of Yahweh for his people is the unifying
idea of this book. In order to bridge the gap between the
two Testaments the author has used extra-biblical material
where she feels that this would cast light on the biblical
texts and also on the development of biblical theology, for
example, in the chapter on Isaac. Thus, the themes of the
New Testament can be seen as a natural development both
of the Old Testament and of the extra-biblical Jewish traditions.

The same traditions underlie the author's interpretation
of the New Testament text. This extra-biblical material is
found in the *targumim,* that is, the Aramaic translations or
paraphrases of the Old Testament; the *midrashim,* which
are commentaries on the Old Testament; the *Mishnah,* a
collection of oral law committed to writing about 200 A.D.;
and the *Talmud,* the oral law with a commentary attached
to it about 500 A.D. The following books contain some of
the standard English translations of these texts:

Epstein, I., ed., *The Babylonian Talmud.* Soncino, London and
New York, 1938.
Freedman and Simon, trans. and eds., *Midrash Rabbah.* Soncino,
London and New York, 1961.
Danby, H., trans. and ed., *Mishnah.* Oxford University Press, Ox-
ford, 1933.
Goldin, Judah, trans., *The Fathers according to Rabbi Nathan.*
Yale University Press, New Haven, 1955.

The student may not be able to avail himself of these ex-
pensive texts, but one of the following anthologies is indispensable for the reader:

Montefiore, C. G., and H. Loewe, eds., *A Rabbinic Anthology.*
   Harper (Torchbooks), New York, 1960.
Newman, L. J., ed., *A Talmudic Anthology.* Behrman, New York,
   1966.
Cohen, A., *Everyman's Talmud,* rev. ed. Dutton, New York, 1949.

   The Jewish texts mentioned above are difficult to date,
but in their oral form they frequently represent pre-Christian
thought. Modern scholarship, especially by comparing these
texts with the manuscripts discovered near the Dead Sea
from 1947 onward, is tending to date the *targumim, midrashim,* and like materials earlier than previous scholars dared
to claim. The author has felt free to use such material both
to elucidate the New Testament text and its background and
to suggest that we must see our Jewish heritage as one which
contains a rich variety of teaching, much of which approxi-
mates that of Jesus and the early Church. In this way a vital
continuity is seen between Judaism and Christianity.

   This book does not pretend in any way to be complete, but
it does have a methodological approach. The author has
dealt only with the materials a student is capable of assimi-
lating in one semester. Thus, she wished to discuss the
prophetical movement; by experience, however, she realized
that a student at this stage cannot master the whole book of
Jeremiah or Isaiah but will be more satisfied with the smaller
prophetical books. This, at least, will give him a glimpse of
prophecy.

   In the same way, in the New Testament section, the author has used the Gospel of St. Matthew as a basis for discussion, and among her own students has required only this
as a "set" text. However, it is to be expected that the student
will be introduced to a synopsis or harmony of the Gospels
in which the Gospel texts are placed side by side. In this
way, he can see the similarities and dissimilarities between

the evangelists' work and learn some appreciation of the theology of each. Two convenient synopses are the following:

Johnston, Leonard, and Aidan Pickering, eds., *A Harmony of the Gospels.* Sheed and Ward, New York, 1944.

Throckmorton, Burton H., Jr., ed., *Gospel Parallels: A Synopsis of the First Three Gospels.* Nelson, New York, 1961.

A teacher might like to use the following books both for his own information and also to direct the students to other sources of historical and critical material:

Black, Matthew, and H. H. Rowley, eds., *Peake's Commentary on the Bible.* Nelson, Camden, N. J., 1962.

Nelson's Complete Concordance of the Revised Standard Version Bible, compiled under the supervision of John Ellison. Nelson, Camden, N. J., 1957.

Hartman, Louis F., ed., *Encyclopedic Dictionary of the Bible* (a translation and adaptation of A. van den Born's *Bijbels Woordenboek,* 2nd rev. ed., 1954–1957). McGraw-Hill, New York, 1963.

Richardson, Alan, *A Theological Word Book of the Bible.* Macmillan, New York, 1957 (paperback).

Vermes, Geza, *The Dead Sea Scrolls in English.* Penguin Books, Baltimore, 1962.

Anderson, B. W., *Understanding the Old Testament.* Prentice-Hall, Englewood Cliffs, N. J., 1966.

Davies, W. D., *An Invitation to the New Testament.* Doubleday, Garden City, 1967.

It is hoped that this book might give the students a love for sacred scripture, present biblical theology as meaningful for their lives, increase their respect for their Jewish heritage, and present Jesus as a true Semite and a historical character.

Only a man of understanding, who can join rope to rope, can draw from a deep well [the Law] full of water.

Canticles Rabbah XCIII

I THE OLD TESTAMENT

1 The Beginning of Biblical Election

Perhaps it would be better if the bible's two major divisions were called the Former *Contract* and the Latter *Contract,* instead of the Old *Testament* and the New *Testament.* The whole of biblical history is woven around the idea of a mutual and definitive relationship formed between God and man, which today, perhaps, we should call a "contract." The bible is the history of the way in which God and man drew themselves together (*contraho,* to draw together) and maintained their union.

Let us first turn to the Old Testament to discover more precisely what is meant by covenant or contract. First we shall examine some different forms of covenant between human beings, and then we shall see this relationship lifted to a higher level and used to consolidate God's relationship to man and man's to God.

"Covenant" (*berith* in Hebrew) means an agreement, pact, or treaty between two parties which sets up a special relationship, a bond of communion. One may have a covenant of parity, which is between equals, or a covenant of suzerainty, which is between a superior and an inferior, for example, between a king and a conquered nation.

SECULAR COVENANTS

In Genesis and the rest of the bible we find several covenants of parity, sometimes made over quite secular matters.

3

If we read Genesis 21:25–34, we find Abraham and Abimelech, king of Gerar, making an agreement or covenant over
a well. Abimelech's servants had seized the water, and Abraham wished to secure this vital commodity for his own
people. The two chiefs did not draw up a document and
sign it before witnesses but did as follows:

So Abraham took sheep and oxen and gave them to Abimelech
and the two men made a covenant. Abraham set seven ewe lambs
of the flock apart. And Abimelech said to Abraham, "What is the
meaning of these seven ewe lambs which you have set apart?"
He said, "These seven ewe lambs you will take from my hand,
that you may be a witness for me that I dug this well." Therefore
that place was called Beersheba; because there both of them
swore an oath. So they made a covenant at Beersheba (Gen.
21:27–32).

In this short extract we can see the basic elements of cove-
nant-making. The matter to be decided on was the well of
water and who would use it. The arrangement was made by
two parties, and the outward signs of this agreement were
the setting aside of the seven ewe lambs and the acceptance
of these lambs by Abimelech. By accepting this gift, according to ancient custom, Abimelech showed in a concrete
way that he recognized Abraham's just claim to the well.
When the ceremony was concluded, a bond of loyalty had
been established between Abraham and his party, on the
one hand, and Abimelech and his party, on the other. To the
ancient man (especially the Semite), to violate such a contract or to sever this loyalty would be unspeakably wrong,
would bring deep shame upon the offender, and would put
him in danger of dire punishments from the deity.

If we read a little further in Genesis, we find another
covenant between Isaac (Abraham's son) and Abimelech

which appears as a kind of sequel to the earlier covenant between Abraham and Abimelech. This covenant was also preceded by certain quarrels about a well. Abimelech then approached Isaac:

We see plainly that the Lord is with you; so we say, let there be an oath between you and us, and let us make a covenant with you, that you will do us no harm, just as we have not touched you and have done to you nothing but good and have sent you away in peace. You are now the blessed of the Lord (Gen. 26:28–29).

These words of Abimelech bring out one of the outstanding characteristics of many covenants, namely, the fact that the two parties become sacrosanct to one another—they would do no harm to one another. It also brings to our attention another outward sign which frequently accompanied the making of a covenant, namely, the partaking of a meal together.

So he [Abimelech] made them a feast, and they ate and drank. In the morning they rose early and took oath with one another; and Isaac set them on their way, and they departed from him in peace (Gen. 26:30–31).

The partaking of a common meal was of deep religious significance to ancient man. The sharing of the common principle of life-preservation brought in its wake an appreciation of the interdependence of men and the products of the created world, and it formed a quasi-ontological union so that the participants were regarded as "brothers." As such each owed the other respect and immunity from harm. So the Psalmist speaks in horror of

Even my bosom friend in whom I trusted,
who ate of my bread, [who] has lifted his heel against me
(Ps. 41:9; *compare* Jn. 13:18).

The union was not unlike the dependence of a foetus attached to the placenta in its mother's uterus.

In Genesis 31:44–55 we find a more complicated covenant. Jacob, Isaac's son, had worked for seven years as a hired servant of Laban, his mother's father (Gen. 28:22), to gain Laban's daughter, Rachel, for his wife, but these years

. . . seemed to him but a few days because of the love he had for her (Gen. 29:20).

However, Laban behaved craftily with Jacob and gave Leah, his elder daughter, to him in marriage, instead of Rachel, and Jacob was obliged to work another seven years for Rachel. After being cheated over his salary by Laban several times, Jacob fled from the house of his father-in-law and took with him his two wives, his cattle, and all his flocks. Laban pursued him but was warned by God in a dream (Gen. 31:24) that he must not do any evil to Jacob. When Laban did reach Jacob, he reproached the fugitive because he went away secretly instead of allowing his master to dismiss him from hired service with the customary ceremonies and joy.

Why did you flee secretly, and cheat me, and did not tell me, so that I might have sent you away with mirth and songs, with tambourine and lyre? (Gen. 31:27).

According to contemporary custom Jacob's children would have belonged to Laban (*v.* 43) in his capacity as Jacob's master. Nevertheless, because of the fear of God and because

God's blessing rested on Jacob, as was manifested in Jacob's prosperity, Laban acquiesced and made a covenant with his son-in-law. The promises made in the covenant, namely, that Jacob should not ill-treat his wives or take further wives and so reduce Leah's and Rachel's marital rights, were accompanied by outward signs: first, a heap of stones as a memorial of the covenant, and second, a sacrifice and a meal. But there is one more important point about this covenant, namely, that God was called to witness the promises and the oath was sworn in the name of the Fear of Isaac, that is, the God of Isaac. This covenant has an air of "other-worldliness" about it.

But perhaps the covenant most illustrative of the idea of the sacrosanctity of the agreement is the one which we meet in Joshua 9. This was a case where, even when there was clear deception by one of the parties to the covenant, the promise still remained inviolable. When Joshua and the Israelites entered Canaan after wandering in the desert for forty years, Joshua conquered the cities of Jericho and Ai, and the local inhabitants of Gibeon became anxious that they might suffer a similar fate. So they pretended that they were travelers; they asked Joshua and the elders of the Israelites to make a covenant with them so that they would not be destroyed. This the Israelites did. In three days the Israelites learned that they had been deceived. The mass of the people wished to destroy the Gibeonites, but

. . . the leaders said to all the congregation, "We have sworn to them by the Lord, the God of Israel, and now we may not touch them. This we will do to them, and let them live, lest wrath be upon us, because of the oath which we swore to them." And the leaders said to them, "Let them live." So they became hewers of wood and drawers of water for all the congregation, as the leaders had said of them (Josh. 9:19–21).

This covenant shows the seriousness with which the Semitic people regarded an oath. They would even keep a covenant with those who intentionally deceived them.

We will look at one more secular covenant before we turn to the covenants between God and man. In I Samuel 18:1–4 we find a covenant between Jonathan, the son of King Saul, and David. Jonathan clothed David with his own garments and armor; David probably gave him his in exchange. Thereby, the two men symbolically intermingled their personalities, for clothes were regarded as an extension of one's personality. Hence, they established between themselves a special bond or relationship.

... the soul of Jonathan was knit to the soul of David, and Jonathan loved him as his own soul. ... Then Jonathan made a covenant with David, because he loved him as his own soul. And Jonathan stripped himself of the robe that was upon him, and gave it to David, and his armor, and even his sword and his bow and his girdle (1 Sam. 18:1–4).

Among some nations it is still a custom to interchange clothing with all its perspiration and dust, thereby symbolizing the interchange of the essence of life, thus knitting the one personality to the other. *Mutatis mutandis,* it is the same in marriage, when one gives a ring, or at the ordination of a priest or the coronation of a king or a queen, when the vestments used dynamically symbolize the new characteristics and functions which the recipients assume. When Jonathan had made the covenant with David, he regarded David's safety above loyalty to the king, his father. Thus, when Saul persecuted David, Jonathan did all he could to enable David to save his life and escape (1 Sam. 20). This covenant impresses on our minds the quality of *hesed,* that is, love and faithfulness, which is the essential quality of the bonds cemented in a covenant relationship.

All these covenants show how ancient man formed special bonds of relationship with his fellows, how an outward ceremony accompanied the swearing of that bond, and how a sacrosanct character sealed the relationship thus established. Perhaps this relationship is expressed best by the "knitting together" of soul and soul as in the last covenant. God's interest, witness, and part in the covenant is illustrated in several cases, for example, Genesis 31 and 1 Samuel 18. God is witness to this solemn act and will punish the party who violates it.

When God wished to establish a similar relationship between himself and man, he used this cultural medium through which to express and ratify that relationship. He knew that a man would understand an experience which he had frequently undergone with his fellowmen.

SPIRITUAL COVENANTS

When we turn to spiritual covenants, first we can take as an example the covenant between God and Noah (Gen. 6). The earth had grown corrupt, and God decided to destroy all flesh on the earth by a great flood. Before the flood he chose a man called Noah and his family and made them the special object of his predilection and determined to rescue them from the impending catastrophe. Therefore, God said,

For behold, I will bring a flood of waters upon the earth, to destroy all flesh in which is the breath of life from under heaven; everything that is on the earth shall die. But I will establish my covenant with you; and you shall come into the ark, you, your sons, your wife, and your sons' wives with you (Gen. 6:17–18).

The covenant was initiated by God and on his side was the gracious condescension to save Noah and his family and a sign of his personal interest in a particular man; on Noah's side only the construction of the ark and obedience to God were required. In Genesis 9 we find the end of this narrative. God established another covenant with Noah. He increased his promises to Noah by extending them to his descendants and also to the animal world.

Behold, I establish my covenant with you and your descendants after you. . . . I establish my covenant with you, that never again shall all flesh be cut off by the waters of a flood, and never again shall there be a flood to destroy the earth (Gen. 9:8–11).

God added an external sign, the rainbow.

When the bow is in the clouds, I will look upon it and remember the everlasting covenant between God and every living creature of all flesh that is upon the earth (Gen. 9:16).

THE COVENANT WITH ABRAHAM

But all these covenants look pale beside the great covenant which God established between himself and Abraham and Sarah. Genesis 15 is the most dramatic, poignant, and dynamic covenant until we come to the Eucharist. In Genesis 15 the bible portrays God speaking to Abraham. Abraham expressed his anxiety about his childlessness because his heir was to be Eliezer of Damascus, his servant and slave, whom he was going to adopt as his son. God reassured Abraham that a child would be born to him and that he would give Abraham the land of Canaan.

God confirmed this promise by an almost unbelievable covenant ceremony. He told Abraham to take a heifer, a she-goat, and a ram, to cut the animals up, and to place them in two lines so that a lane was formed between them. Abraham protected the carcasses from the birds of prey. At sunset Abraham fell into a trance, and "lo, a dread and great darkness fell upon him" (Gen. 15:12). Then God uttered the precise terms of the covenant.

Know of a surety that your descendants will be sojourners in a land that is not theirs, and will be slaves there, and they will be oppressed for four hundred years; but I will bring judgment on the nation which they serve, and afterward they shall come out with great possessions (Gen. 15:12–14).

God not only promised Abraham descendants but also foretold that they would be captive in Egypt and that he would rescue them from there. God not only took thought for Abraham's immediate son, Isaac, but promised to step into the course of history and deliver his descendants in order to keep his covenant. Then a most arresting event occurred.

When the sun had gone down and it was dark, behold, a smoking fire pot and a flaming torch passed between these pieces (Gen. 15:17).

When men used this form of covenant—a covenant of pieces with a fellowman—each man swearing the covenant walked through the lane formed by the animals and, by so doing, indicated that he was prepared to go to death and be destroyed like the animals rather than break the covenant; if he did break the covenant, he expected to be destroyed like the animals.[1] But in this case it was God, not Abraham, who

---

[1] T. H. Robinson, *Zeitschrift für die alttestamentliche Wissenschaft,* 42 (1924), pp. 20–21, has suggested that the party passing through the lane symbolically entered the slaughtered victim.

walked through the lane and made these promises. The smoking fire pot and the flaming torch in Abraham's trance are symbols of God himself. God showed Abraham that he took this covenant as seriously as any human person could and, although God in his very nature cannot be destroyed or killed by men, he promised that in order to keep this covenant he himself would go to the point of death.

To Christians, who believe that God took human flesh in Jesus Christ, who would die, this covenant is of unique surpassing importance. If Abraham could have looked forward, he would have seen that God kept his promise. In order to fulfill in all seriousness the covenant with his people, God died on the cross.

According to extra-biblical writing the Jewish people did believe that Abraham had a vision of the future and that he was shown "someone" who would be taken as a pledge for the people. When Jesus said, "Your father Abraham rejoiced that he was to see my day; he saw it and was glad" (Jn. 8:5), he may have been alluding to this Jewish belief.

But the bible only tells us that in that vision Abraham believed that God would accomplish three things: (1) God would give him descendants; (2) God would give his descendants the land of Canaan; (3) God would rescue the children of Israel from the land of Egypt.

And he believed the Lord; and he reckoned it to him as righteousness (Gen. 15:6).

This was a tremendous event in biblical history, for God himself entered into a covenant relationship with Abraham under the forms which among his fellowmen guaranteed the most inviolable security. The solemnity of the covenants, which we have seen in those between Abraham and Abimelech, Joshua and the Gibeonites, David and Jonathan, is now seen to apply to the God of heaven and earth, the creator of man and woman.

In Genesis 17:1–14 Abraham experienced another theophany, that is, another appearance of the deity. God said to him,

. . . I am God almighty; walk before me, and be blameless. And I will make my covenant between me and you, and will multiply you exceedingly.

And Abraham fell on his face. We shall often find this action following a theophany; it is a very useful detail supplied by the biblical compiler because it confirms that the subject experienced a very special revelation from God (*compare* Jn. 18:6).

Chapter 17 in Genesis may deal with another covenant between Abraham and God, or it may be an extended discussion of the one in Genesis 15. In Chapter 17 God confirmed his promise to Abraham that he would have a son, but he magnified the promise by saying that Abraham would be "the father of a multitude of nations" (*v.* 4) and kings would come forth from him. As an earnest of this promise God changes Abraham's name from "Abram," which means "exalted father," to "Abraham," which means "father of a multitude." Both the promise of numerous descendants and the change of one's name was of high significance to the Semitic man. Descendants were important to him because at that time he had little or no concept of life after death, so his immortality lay in producing children. A change of name symbolized an essential change in one's innermost being, almost in one's essence.

Moreover, in this covenant God put an obligation on Abraham and his descendants.

Every male among you shall be circumcised. You shall be circumcised in the flesh of your foreskins, and it shall be a sign of the covenant between me and you (Gen. 17:10–11).

Circumcision was, and still is of course, a widespread practice among many people, but the uniqueness of the Hebrew practice lay in the fact that it was performed, not as a prenuptial or an adolescent rite, but when the child was eight days old. It was a visible sign of the purity which was indispensable for intimate communion with God.

The sign of the covenant has been faithfully kept by the Jews throughout all ages; in the Christian dispensation it has been superseded by baptism, which in the time of Christ was the feminine initiation rite into Judaism. Christianity, by this change, implicitly showed that man and woman have equal rights, graces, and responsibilities before God. But even in this Old Testament chapter God thinks of women. After making a requirement which applied only to the male (there is no history of female circumcision in Judaism), God turned his attention to Sarah. He treated her in exactly the same way as he had Abraham. He changed her name or character, and she became not "Sarai" but "Sarah." Sarah probably means princess. Then he gave her the blessing of fertility; this was a manifest miracle after so many years of childlessness: a promise identical to the one made to Abraham was given to her.

I will bless her, and moreover I will give you a son by her; I will bless her, and she shall be a mother of nations; kings of peoples shall come from her (Gen. 17:16).

Abraham did not believe God at first, and he laughed at the idea of a man of one hundred years and a woman of ninety giving birth to a child. But God was not pleased with his mirth and insisted,

No, but Sarah your wife shall bear you a son, and you shall call his name Isaac. I will establish my covenant with him as an everlasting covenant for his descendants after him. As for Ishmael, I have heard you; behold, I will bless him and make him fruitful and multiply him exceedingly; he shall be the father of twelve princes, and I will make him a great nation. But I will establish my covenant with Isaac, whom Sarah shall bear to you at this season (Gen. 17:19–21).

This chapter sets the stage for the whole of salvation history. Here God selected not only a particular man but also a particular woman to be the vehicle of his promises throughout the ages. It was not sufficient for God that Abraham should have a child, Ishmael, through Hagar, Sarah's handmaid, even though, according to the custom of the day, Hagar was an extension of the personality of Sarah and hence a child born through her was regarded as Sarah's child. God insisted that Sarah herself should give birth to the heir of the covenant between Abraham and God.

This insistence of God also seems to be behind the mysterious stories of the abduction of Sarah and Rachel in Genesis 12:10–20, 20:1–18 and 26:6–11.[2] Abraham did not appear to think that it was important to preserve Sarah; rather, he thought of preserving his own life so that the promise of posterity might be fulfilled. Perhaps he thought that his son Ishmael was sufficient for the fulfillment of God's promise or that God would give him another wife. He did not appear to understand that the promises of God were made only to

[2] See E. A. Speiser, *Genesis, The Anchor Bible* (New York, 1964), pp. 91–94.

Sarah. God rescued Sarah and intervened miraculously on her part as he did later for Rachel, Tamar, Ruth, and other women who were chosen vessels. Salvation history was never solely a male affair; it was always a family affair.

2 The Man Whom God Elected

Now that we have seen God's great condescension in making a contract or covenant with mankind, let us look at the background of the man and woman whom God chose.

ABRAHAM'S RELIGIOUS BACKGROUND

The bible tells us that Abraham's descendants came from Mesopotamia, a pagan environment (*circa* 2000-1700 B.C.).

. . . Your fathers lived of old beyond the Euphrates, Terah the father of Abraham and of Nahor; and they served other gods. (Josh. 24:2).

If we look into the religious and cultural background of Abraham,[1] we are astounded at the stark contrast between the religion which he adopted and that of his ancestors. Religious life in Ur was, of course, completely pagan. Sumerian texts mention about five thousand names of gods. Even if one god might have more than one name, this was polytheism at its height. The chief sanctuary, both at Ur and Haran, was dedicated to the moon-god, Sin. There still remains in the city of Ur a famous ziggurat, which probably

---

[1] The traditions concerning Abraham may, of course, belong to a tribe rather than to one man.

belonged to Sin. A ziggurat is a temple tower like the tower of Babel which the people tried to build (Gen. 11:1–9). Other gods appear to have been arranged in a kind of hierarchy around Sin. From cylinder seals, with which people sealed their letters and legal documents, we can see the owner of the seal introduced to one of the leading gods. The picture signifies the citizen of Ur showing his allegiance to the god of the city.

We find one quite concrete link between the moon cult and Abraham's ancestors, for Abraham's father was called Terah, and this name "Terah" happens to be another name for the moon-god. This name is found in North Syria at a place called Ras Shamra, where many ancient tablets were found. So, it does seem that Abraham's family was connected with the moon cult. Such, therefore, was the probable religious background of Abraham, the originator of the Jewish religion.

In nonbiblical Jewish tradition there is a story which is constantly repeated about Abraham. It tells how Abraham's father told his son to go to the marketplace in Ur and sell idols. But Abraham did not make much profit, for he told everyone who came to his stall that the idols were useless; they were not really gods. Abraham's father became very angry and determined to punish his son who appeared to be rebellious to his father, to the gods, and to the king, all of whom in those days were intimately related as regards the honor due to them. Terah, Abraham's father, handed him over to Nimrod, the great hunter, chief of the area, and Nimrod cast him into a fiery furnace. But to everyone's surprise Abraham walked out completely unscathed. Later Jews attributed this to Abraham's belief in the true God. Abraham's brother, Haran, thought he would try fire-walking as well but he was burnt to death because he did not believe in the true God.

This story does not appear to have a kernel of historical truth in it, but its theological aspect is important. Among the Jews there was an ancient and strong tradition that while Abraham was in Ur, there began to dawn on him the realization that the pagan gods of Ur were not real but that there was a supreme being who was. The Jewish people believed that this concept came to Abraham through special divine revelation.

Against this background it is easier to see the election of Abraham which is recorded in Genesis 12; this is perhaps one of the most important texts in the bible since it is concerned with the beginning and essence of biblical election. God appeared to Abraham and said,

Go from your country and your kindred and your father's house to the land that I will show you. And I will make of you a great nation, and I will bless you, and make your name great, so that you will be a blessing. I will bless those who bless you, and him who curses you I will curse; and by you [or in you] all the families of the earth shall bless themselves (Gen. 12:1–3).

Through this command God called Abraham away from pagan surroundings and culture and away from his family, who were idol worshipers.

Pagan gods were, in some mysterious way, supposed to be attached to the soil of the land in which they were worshiped, almost like a king who reigns only over a particular area. On leaving an area one could take his household gods with him, or adopt other gods in his new homeland, or take with him some of the soil of the land. Naaman, the Syrian, whom Elisha the Prophet cured of leprosy did this.

Then Naaman said, "If not [if you will not receive a present], I pray to you, let there be given your servant two mules' burden of earth; for henceforth your servant will not offer burnt offering or sacrifice to any god but the Lord. In this matter may the Lord pardon your servant; when my master goes into the house of Rimmon to worship there, leaning on my arm, and I bow myself in the house of Rimmon, when I bow myself in the house of Rimmon, the Lord pardon your servant in this matter." He said to him, "Go in peace" (2 Kings 5:17–19).

When Abraham and his wife migrated, they were able to move out of the influence and obligation of the pagan gods of their fathers. They could have adopted the gods of the land of Canaan, but Abraham had decided not to.

ABRAHAM'S RELIGIOUS BELIEF

This was a momentous decision. We do not necessarily believe that Abraham had reached the stage of religious evolution where one believes in only one god (monotheism), but the texts do show that he and his family worshiped only one god (monolatry). Belief in one god was to evolve about the time of Moses, or even after that. But Abraham did adopt a cult, which was unique in many respects.

Abraham's God was very different from the gods in his new surroundings. His neighbors must have thought this group of seminomad shepherds very odd people indeed. First of all, Abraham had no name for his God; he was just "the Lord." God's name was to be revealed later to Moses (Ex. 3:13–15). By giving his God no name Abraham implicitly acknowledged that he did not understand the nature of God or have any power over him. To the Semite, to name something or someone was to indicate that one knew something of the character of that person or something about his birth or history. To know the name of someone was also to have some possession of his nature or some power or influence with his being. We understand this idea when we remember the devils who revealed their names and were cast out of the possessed people (Mk. 5:1–20). This lack of a name also indicated that Abraham's God was not a god of one area or territory, such as Ur, or over one natural phenomenon, such as the sun or the moon, or over a special power of nature, such as the harvest, or over a special activity of man, such as battle or love, or the personification of such phenomena. Abraham's God had authority over the whole universe; in fact, according to nonbiblical Jewish tradition, the Jews expressed the belief that it was with Abraham that men and women first began to acknowledge a God of both heaven and earth. Before that no one had conceived of such a being.

Abraham's God also had another peculiarity. He was neither male nor female. The pagans thought in human capacities, and for them a god must have a consort, and a goddess, a husband. But this God was neither male nor female, and because of this, men's minds were obliged to rise at least to a minimal level of philosophical or metaphysical thought in order to conceive of this God, who is purely spirit, an incorporeal being, completely unfettered by human activities and limitations, free from human caprice and emotions, and above all immortal—for the predication of sex to the pagan gods to some extent implied that they, like man, must gain immortality through procreation. This metaphysical concept was probably realized even more by Moses at the incident of the burning bush.[2]

With this peculiar concept of God, Abraham and his family became wandering nomads in the land of Canaan.

[2] See Chapter 5.

Perhaps this very wandering enabled them to keep their unique concept of God. It kept them as a fairly exclusive community; they even married within their clan (Gen. 24:3–9; 28:1–5).

We must take one more look at Genesis 12:1–3. In this text there are five special points. First, separation from paganism is required of Abraham. Second, a promise of posterity is given to him. Third, Abraham is elected as a mediator of blessing to others: "by you shall all the families of the earth be blessed"; this "missionary aspect" was quite new for it was not common among ancient religions except as a political stratagem, employed to subdue a people to a state. Fourth, in verse three is found the genesis of salvation and judgment: men will be judged by their attitude and conduct toward God's chosen vessel, Abraham, and his descendants and the religion embodied in them. Fifth, this blessing and cursing is not confined to the Israelites but extends to all mankind, that is, Abraham is to spread a universal religion. By this very means—a common, grace-bearing, vivifying religion—Abraham will recreate a unity among men.

In fact the promise made to Abraham is fulfilled in Christianity, as is seen in Acts 3:25–26, Romans 4:13, and Galatians 3:8–16. Abraham's work is to be the reversal of the situation in Genesis 11:1–9 when men tried to build a tower to the God of the skies, a ziggurat like the one dedicated to the moon-god.

And the Lord said, "Behold, they are one people, and they have all one language; and this is only the beginning of what they will do; and nothing that they propose to do will now be impossible for them. Come, let us go down, and there confuse their language, that they may not understand one another's speech." So the Lord scattered them abroad from there over the face of all the earth, and they left off building the city (Gen. 11::6–9).

This story means that God wished men to realize that they are not "self-made." To Abraham, who realized this, God gave the responsibility of this missionary work, which would lead men again to unity. This type of unity was concretely illustrated in Acts 2:1–47 when for a brief time a unity of language was established.

The covenant between God and Abraham and Abraham's descendants was time and again in jeopardy. We have only to think of the abduction of Sarah and Rachel, the matriarchs, or their sterility or the division of the land between Lot and Abraham (Gen. 13:12–18). In this last instance, Lot chose the best land and then went to dwell among the cities of the Jordan valley; there he encountered the corruption of the cities and escaped destruction only due to the help of an angel and the intercession of Abraham (Gen. 19). But throughout the history recorded in the Old Testament, just when the hopes of the Israelites are lowest and when they think that they are to be exterminated, God comes to their rescue in virtue of the covenant which he has "cut" with them. Two of these occasions are recorded in the following chapters. We turn to the first of them now, the sacrifice of Isaac by his father, Abraham.

FURTHER READING

Holt, John M., *The Patriarchs of Israel*. Vanderbilt University Press, Nashville, 1964.

Hunt, Ignatius, *The World of the Patriarchs*. Prentice-Hall, Englewood Cliffs, N.J., 1967.

Woolley, L., *Abraham, Recent Discoveries in Hebrew Origins*. Faber and Faber, London, 1936.

——— *Ur of the Chaldees*. Norton, New York, 1965 (paperback).

De Vaux, R. "Les patriarchs Hébreux et les Découvertes Modernes." *Revue Biblique* 53 (1946), pp. 321-348.

3 The First Savior

In Genesis 22 we find a curious incident. It is a narrative which is one of the most beautifully told in any literature: simple, dramatic, and deeply religious.

After these things God tested Abraham, and said to him, "Abraham!" And he said. "Here am I." He said, "Take your son, your only son Isaac, whom you love, and go to the land of Moriah, and offer him there as a burnt offering upon one of the mountains of which I shall tell you" (Gen. 22:1–2).

THE NATURE OF ISAAC'S SACRIFICE

Scholars have tried to decide how this episode came about. Some have suggested that the incident manifests that Abraham was still influenced by paganism. He thought his God required human sacrifice, and not only human sacrifice, but the destruction, total immolation, of the one promised son, who had been born as the heir to the promises after so many years of waiting by Abraham and his wife, Sarah. Others suggest that this narrative is recorded by the compiler of Genesis to show that the God of Abraham was different from pagan gods because, in reality, he did not require human sacrifice. This may indeed be true. It is quite credible as a historical event that Abraham thought God wanted this sacrifice, but at the very moment immediately before his accomplishment of the sacrifice divine revelation taught him that this was not so. Human sacrifices, however, were practiced in the Semitic world.

When the king of Moab saw that the battle was going against him, he took with him seven hundred swordsmen to break through, opposite the king of Edom; but they could not. Then he took his eldest son who was to reign in his stead, and offered him for a burnt offering upon the wall. And there came great wrath upon Israel; and they withdrew from him and returned to their own land (2 Kings 3:26–27).

Other scholars have understood this story of Abraham and Isaac as an etiological narrative because it explains the name of the place, Moriah—"the Lord will provide." Indeed, the Lord provided a ram to be sacrificed instead of Isaac.

But to the Jewish commentators, ancient and modern, the story of Isaac had a far greater theological significance and, as Professor Vermes comments, it "played a prominent part in the doctrinal development of Judaism."[1]

Indeed, if we study the Jewish writers carefully we can see that the narrative of Isaac, which they called the Binding (*akedah*), not only showed the perfect love and obedience of Abraham but also demonstrated that Isaac's sacrifice was voluntary, that it was a sacrifice which wrought atonement.

In a Targum, which is an Aramaic paraphrase of an Old Testament passage, the following version of the story of Isaac appears:

And Abraham said: "The Word of the Lord shall prepare a lamb

[1] G. Vermes, *Scripture and Tradition in Judaism* (E. J. Brill, Leiden, 1961), p. 19, used with permission.

for Himself. If not, my son, you shall be the burnt offering."
And they went together with a quiet heart (22:8).

Abraham stretched out his hand and took the knife to kill Isaac
his son. Isaac answered and said to Abraham his father: "Bind
my hands properly that I may not struggle in the time of my pain
and disturb you and render your offering unfit and be cast into
the pit of destruction in the world to come." The eyes of Abraham
were turned to the eyes of Isaac but the eyes of Isaac were
turned to the angels of heaven. Isaac saw them but Abraham did
not see them. In that hour the angels of heaven went out and
said to each other: "Let us go and see the only two just men
in the world. The one slays, and the other is being slain. The
slayer does not hesitate, and the one being slain stretches out his
neck" (22:10).

Abraham worshipped and prayed the Name of the Word of the
Lord, and said: "O Lord, You are He that sees and is unseen! I
pray: all is revealed before You. It is known before You that there
was no division in my heart at the time when You told me to
offer Isaac my son, and to make him dust and ashes before You.
But I departed immediately in the morning and did Your word
with joy and fulfilled it. Now I pray for mercy before You, O
Lord God, that when the children of Isaac come to a time of
distress, You may remember on their behalf the binding of Isaac
their father, and loose and forgive them their sins and deliver
them from all distress, so that the generations which follow him
may say: In the mountain of the Temple of the Lord, Abraham
offered Isaac his son, and in this mountain—of the Temple—the
glory of the Shekhinah of the Lord was revealed to him"
(22:14).[2]

Here we note details additional to those given us by the
biblical narrator. First, Abraham told Isaac that he would be

[2] *Ibid.*, pp. 194–195.

sacrificed; second, Isaac consented; third, Isaac received a vision; and fourth, Abraham prayed that the suffering of himself and of Isaac would bring good in the future to the children of Isaac. These additions change the story: Isaac's sacrifice is the result of his own free will, and Abraham's prayer gives the sacrifice a vicarious aspect, that is, it is suffered on behalf of others.

As time progressed, the Jewish teachers and writers stressed the consent of Isaac even more. One important rabbi near the time of Christ said,

You shall love the Lord your God . . . with all your soul like Isaac who bound himself upon the altar.

Later writers describe Isaac as running with joy to the altar. In a book called the Fourth Book of the Maccabees, Isaac is seen as the protomartyr.

All these ideas meant that the sacrifice was no longer viewed as a test of Abraham's faith but rather as Isaac's voluntary sacrifice. Indeed, these elaborations reached such a point that at last the purpose of Isaac's miraculous birth from a nonagenarian was seen as the sanctification of his life by means of his sacrificial death. In one writer, Isaac is made to say,

As though I had been born into this world to be offered in sacrifice to Him who made me . . .

In Vermes' words, "by Isaac's unique example God conferred upon human nature its true dignity, the dignity of a divinely required and freely offered self-sacrifice. The blessing resulting from it would extend to all men for ever, and they would understand that they possess the same humanity

which was made holy by Isaac's sacrifice."[3] We see here that
the Jews had developed the idea of vicarious suffering, death,
and resurrection, but they centered their theology on Isaac,
not on Christ.

Eventually in this Jewish theology of the Binding of
Isaac we find elements of affinity with the Suffering Servant
of Isaiah 53. In Second Isaiah (Chapters 40–55) appear the
songs which are now termed "Servant Songs." These songs
speak of a man of God who will suffer death, although he is
not guilty, and his innocent suffering will bring benefit to all
Israel.

> Surely he has borne our griefs
>   and carried our sorrows;
> yet we esteemed him stricken,
>   smitten by God, and afflicted.
> But he was wounded for our transgressions,
>   he was bruised for our iniquities;
> upon him was the chastisement that made us whole,
>   and with his stripes we are healed. . . .
> when he made himself an offering for sin,
>   he shall see his offspring, he shall prolong his days. . . .
> by his knowledge shall the righteous one, my servant,
>   make many to be accounted righteous;
>   and he shall bear their iniquities (Is. 53:4–5, 10–11).

Both the Suffering Servant and Isaac were regarded as
men who freely offered their lives for others; both were
compared to a lamb (cf. Is. 53:7); and the suffering of both
was thought to bring relief for sinners. In one Aramaic
paraphrase Isaac is actually called the "servant of the
Lord."[4] The theology behind both these figures is the theory

---

[3] *Ibid.*, p. 201.
[4] *Ibid.*, p. 203.

of the atoning and expiatory effect of the blood of a martyr.

Yet there is one major difficulty about the sacrifice of Isaac, and the Jewish teachers did not gloss it over: Isaac did not die and did not shed his blood. Could there really be atoning sacrifice without the shedding of blood? In Leviticus we read,

For the life of the flesh is in the blood; and I have given it for you upon the altar to make atonement for your souls; for it is the blood that makes atonement, by reason of the life (Lev. 17:11).

Thus, the law of the Jews showed that blood was necessary for atonement. The Jewish teachers gave this much thought. Some said that Isaac had the intention to die.

Though he did not die, Scripture credits Isaac with having died and his ashes having lain upon the altar (*Midrash Hagadol*, Gen. 22:19).[5]

God regards the ashes of Isaac as though they were piled upon the altar.[6]

Other commentators said that Isaac shed one fourth of his blood, and therefore atonement could be made.

The Holy One, Blessed be He, said to Moses: I keep faith to pay the reward of Isaac, son of Abraham, who gave one-fourth of his blood on the altar.[7]

Even though these were theories rather than historical facts, they show how eager the Jews were to show that Isaac's sacrifice was a real one.

[5] *Ibid.*, p. 205.
[6] *Ibid.*, p. 205.
[7] *Ibid.*, p. 206.

THE EFFECTS OF ISAAC'S SACRIFICE

Having established that Isaac's sacrifice was a valid vicarious one in the Jewish mind, let us see what effects the Jewish teachers thought the sacrifice wrought. The effects are foreshadowed in Abraham's prayer, which he offered before going to sacrifice Isaac.

Now I pray for mercy before You, O Lord God, that when the children of Isaac come to a time of distress You may remember on their behalf the Binding of Isaac their father and loose and forgive them their sins and deliver them from all distress.

So Abraham prayed for safety and forgiveness. However, the Jews were more specific than this. They believed that four things were granted through the favor of Isaac: first, the first-born sons of the Israelites were saved in Egypt; second, Israel was saved at the Red Sea; third, the Israelites were forgiven for the sins of idolatry which they committed by making and worshiping the golden calf, while Moses was on the Mount of Sinai with God (Ex. 32); and fourth, and most important of all, they believed that through the merits of Isaac the dead would be resurrected.

Through the merits of Isaac, who offered himself upon the altar, the Holy One, blessed be He, shall raise the dead. For it is written [Ps. 102, 19–20] *From heaven the Lord looked upon the earth to hear the groaning of the captive, to deliver the children of death.*[8]

Indeed, Isaac was regarded as the prototype of the resurrected man, for, as it were, he died and came to life again.

[8] *Ibid.*, p. 207.

Vermes gives an excellent summary of the theology of the Binding.

In short, the Binding of Isaac was thought to have played a unique role in the whole economy of the salvation of Israel, and to have a permanent redemptive effect on behalf of its people. The merits of his sacrifice were experienced by the Chosen People in the past, invoked in the present, and hoped for at the end of time.[9]

The Binding of Isaac is not disassociated from the sacrifices in the Temple. Isaac's rescue showed that God did not want human blood but the blood of animals. The Jews saw the sacrifices in the Temple as the fulfillment of God's wish expressed at Moriah. The site of the Temple of Jerusalem was supposed to be the very rock upon which the Binding occurred (Muslims venerate it to this day). Eventually Jerusalem became the only place where it was permitted to offer sacrifice. Jewish writings show that all sacrifices were offered in memory of Isaac's sacrifice, to remind God of this sacrifice and to receive merit. But it was especially the lamb which evoked the memory of Isaac.

The lamb was chosen to recall the merit of the Lamb of Abraham, who bound himself upon the altar and stretched out his neck for Your Name's sake. . . . For this reason he acquired merit and a lamb was provided there, in his stead, for the burnt offering.[10]

The Binding of Isaac was also associated with the Passover, not only because the merit of Isaac was thought to have rescued the first-born sons of the Hebrews but also

---

[9] *Ibid.*, p. 208.
[10] *Ibid.*, p. 211.

because the blood on the doorposts of the Israelite houses reminded God of Isaac's blood.

And when I see the blood, I will pass over you—I see the blood of the Binding of Isaac.[11]

ISAAC AND JESUS

The fully developed theology of vicarious sacrifice and its connection with the Passover was taken over by the writers of the New Testament, but in the place of Isaac they set Jesus Christ. Jesus fulfilled the role which Isaac was unable to fill because he had not actually died and risen.

St. Paul saw the sacrifice of Jesus in terms of the theology of the Binding of Isaac when he spoke of God not sparing his own son, although he had spared Abraham's son.

He who did not spare his own Son but gave him up for us all, will he not also give us all things with him? (Rom. 8:32; *compare* Rom. 5:9).

For St. Paul, the "offspring of Abraham" is Christ rather than Isaac.

Now the promises were made to Abraham and to his offspring. It does not say, "And to offsprings," referring to many; but referring to one, "And to your offspring," which is Christ (Gal. 3:16).

St. Paul calls Jesus the Passover lamb, just as Isaac was connected with the Passover lamb.

[11] *Ibid.*, p. 216.

Cleanse out the old leaven that you may be a new lump, as you really are unleavened. For Christ, our paschal lamb, has been sacrificed (1 Cor. 5:7).

St. Mark may also have had Genesis 22:12 in mind when he wrote in his Gospel, "Thou are my beloved son; with thee I am well pleased" (Mk. 1:11). A more certain reference is found in St. John who recorded St. John the Baptist's exclamation to two of his disciples when they saw Jesus walking by:

Behold, the Lamb of God (Jn. 1:36);

Behold the Lamb of God, who takes away the sin of the world (Jn 1:29; *compare* Rev. 5:12—Worthy is the Lamb who was slain, to receive power and wealth and wisdom and might and honor and glory and blessing!).

The theology of the Binding of Isaac passed directly into the theology of the person of Christ and the Passover, upon which the Eucharist was founded. It is possible that the daily sacrifices of the Temple were gradually superseded by a frequent celebration of the Eucharist. As Professor Vermes says, "The frequent celebration of the Eucharist meal may, therefore, be understood as the introduction into Christianity of this other element of the *Akedah* theology: the perpetual remembrance of the one perfect sacrifice until the Kingdom comes."[12] Thus, in the dramatic narrative of Genesis 22 the coming Savior is foreshadowed.

FURTHER READING

Levi, I., "Le Sacrifice d'Isaac." *Revue des Etudes Juives* 64 (1912), pp. 156 ff.

[12] *Ibid.*, p. 227.

Schoeps, H. J., *Paul,* trans. by Harold Knight. Westminster, Philadelphia, 1961, pp. 141-149.

Vermes, G., *Scripture and Tradition in Judaism.* E. J. Brill, Leiden, 1961, pp. 19-227.

4 The Beginning of Redemption

Isaac, the son of Abraham, and Jacob, the son of Isaac and his wife Rebecca, were inheritors of the promises of God to Abraham. During the days of Jacob there occurred one of those famines which are not rare phenomena in the land of Canaan. Because of the famine, Jacob and his family went to Egypt to reside near Joseph, Jacob's son. He had been sold as a slave to the Egyptians but later rose in power and became one of the chief ministers of the Pharaoh. This seems to have been during the time when Semitic people called the Hyksos ruled over the land of Egypt (*circa* 1700–1500 B.C.). While they were in power, the Jewish immigrants appear to have enjoyed the status of resident aliens and to have prospered in the land. When the Hyksos were conquered about 1590 B.C., the Egyptians came into sovereignty again and displayed a fierce nationalism. Many of the Semitic people, including the descendants of Abraham, seem to have fallen into slavery or serfdom. This is exactly what was foretold to Abraham during the covenant of the pieces.

Then the Lord said to Abram, "Know of a surety that your descendants will be sojourners in a land that is not theirs, and will be slaves there, and they will be oppressed for four hundred years; but I will bring judgment on the nation which they serve, and afterward they shall come out with great possessions" (Gen. 15:13–14).

THE BIBLICAL CONCEPT OF SLAVERY

In order to understand the condition of the Israelites and the importance of God's action in delivering them, we must examine briefly the idea of slavery according to the scriptures. A slave in the strict sense of the word is one deprived of his freedom, at least for a time, one who becomes the property of another man. Some say that the institution of slavery was not practiced in Israel, but it is hard to support this argument in view of the laws concerning slaves in the Old Testament: these laws presuppose slavery.

The Hebrew laws concerning slaves are especially humane compared to those of the surrounding cultures. These laws gave distinct advantage to slaves who were Hebrews, men from the stock of Abraham. For example, in Leviticus we read,

And if your brother becomes poor beside you, and sells himself to you, you shall not make him serve as a slave: and he shall be with you as a hired servant and as a sojourner. He shall serve with you until the year of the jubilee; then he shall go out from you, he and his children with him, and go back to his own family, and return to the possession of his fathers. . . . You shall not rule over him with harshness, but shall fear your God. As for your male and female slaves whom you may have: you may buy male and female slaves from among the nations that are round about you. You may also buy from among the strangers who sojourn with you and their families that are with you, who have been born in your land; and they may be your property. You may bequeath them to your sons after you, to inherit as a possession forever; you may make slaves of them, but over your brethren the people of Israel you shall not rule, one over another, with harshness (Lev. 25: 39–46).

From this text we can see quite vividly the difference between Hebrew and non-Hebrew slaves. Hebrews are to be hired servants, not slaves; they are to be released in the year of jubilee, and they may take their wives and children with them. They are not to be treated with cruelty. But non-Israelite slaves may be bought and then handed on as an inheritance to their master's heirs. These slaves could, therefore, become permanent slaves and thus fall into a lower status in society, since they are politically and economically at a disadvantage because they have lost the dignity of free persons.

Another text in Leviticus deals with the case of Israelites sold to resident aliens in their own land. Even here the Israelite is regarded as a privileged person and the non-Israelite master is supposed to treat him as such.

If a stranger or sojourner with you becomes rich, and your brother beside him becomes poor and sells himself to the stranger or sojourner with you, or to a member of the stranger's family, then after he is sold he may be redeemed; one of his brothers may redeem him, or his uncle, or his cousin may redeem him, or a kinsman belonging to his family may redeem him; or if he grows rich he may redeem himself. He shall reckon with him who bought him from the year when he sold himself to him until the year of jubilee, and the price of his release shall be according to the number of years; the time he was with his owner shall be rated as the time of a hired servant. If there are still many years, according to them he shall refund out of the price paid for him the price for his redemption. If there remain but a few years until the year of jubilee, he shall make a reckoning with him; according to the years of service due from him he shall refund the money for his redemption. As a servant hired year by year shall he be with him; he shall not rule with harshness over him in your sight. And if he is not redeemed by these means, then he shall be released in the year of jubilee, he and his children with him (Lev. 25:47–54).

From this text we see that the Israelites appear to have expected even a pagan owner to comply with their rules concerning slavery; they also expected the Israelite relatives to redeem the slave or the slave to redeem himself. Very little seems to be said about the rights of the owner; for example, should he wish to keep the slave, what could he do?

These texts reveal the concept of appreciation of the idea of election which the Israelites recognized in themselves. There was an acute awareness of their unique position; they regarded themselves as the privileged people. A relative had not only the right but the duty to redeem his enslaved kinsman and to recover him for his original family and land. In order to redeem himself a man was obliged to work about three years and collect thirty shekels; this might not have been always possible.

If a man were captive in a foreign land, he might have hoped to be ransomed by a powerful friend or relative or their representatives. These representatives would have had to show their credentials; they had to be a certain age and were selected with care for their fitness; it was not unusual for a group of people to go. The matter of redemption was taken very seriously, for unjust enslavement was considered as equivalent to murder.

GOD, THE REDEEMER OF THE JEWS

Against this background we can understand the position of the children of Israel and their redemption by God from

Egypt. God as the special "relative" of Israel, for Israel is regarded as his first-born son in virtue of his covenant with Abraham, is bound to ransom his people. In Exodus, God tells Moses,

And you shall say to Pharaoh, "Thus says the Lord, Israel is my first-born son, and I say to you, 'Let my son go that he may serve me'; if you refuse to let him go, behold, I will slay your first-born son" (Ex. 4:22–23).

God is represented in this text as abiding by the old law of the *lex talionis*, the law of retaliation or exact retribution.

He who kills a man shall be put to death. He who kills a beast shall make it good, life for life. When a man causes disfigurement in his neighbor, as he has done it shall be done to him, fracture for fracture, eye for eye, tooth for tooth (Lev. 24:17–20).

God as the relative of Israel will exact vengeance if Pharaoh will not free his son. These are not the only verses in the Exodus narrative which allow us to see that the compiler was speaking and thinking in legal terms. He saw the enslavement of the Israelites as a direct flouting of social customs and legal enactments by the Pharaoh. In Exodus 1:11 and 13 we find the technical terms "afflict" and "with rigor."

Therefore they [the Egyptians] set taskmasters over them to afflict them with heavy burdens; and they built for Pharaoh store-cities, Pithom and Raamses. . . . They made the people of Israel serve with rigor (Ex. 1:11, 13).

"Afflict" is a legal term meaning to mete out unjust treatment. For example, one speaks of "afflicting a widow" (Ex. 22:22), or Sarah "afflicts" Hagar. "With rigor" means "with harsh treatment"; it is not only injustice but also cruelty.

Then, the term "cry" also appears. A cry is an appeal for justice. Thus one "cries" or appeals to a king for justice (2 Sam. 19:29), or one "cries" to another for help (Judg. 12:2). Perhaps one of the most memorable appeals is the blood of Abel crying to heaven for justice (Gen. 4:10). So in the same way, the Israelites "cry" or appeal to God for justice.

In the course of those many days the king of Egypt died. And the people of Israel groaned under their bondage, and cried for help, and their cry under bondage came up to God (Ex. 2:23).

It is this "cry" which made God recall his covenant.

And God heard their groaning, and God remembered his covenant with Abraham, with Isaac, and with Jacob. And God saw the people of Israel, and God knew (Ex. 2:24).

It was then that God determined to "bring them out" (Ex. 3:8). "To go out" is a technical term for the dismissal of a slave. A slave "goes out" in his seventh year; a daughter who is sold by her father has special privileges in regard to her "going out." This "going out" is accompanied by ceremonies. This is the meaning behind Laban's reproach to Jacob because Jacob had fled secretly from his master instead of going through the usual ceremonies of departure.

And Laban said to Jacob, "What have you done, that you have cheated me, and carried away my daughters like captives of the sword? Why did you flee secretly, and cheat me, and did not tell me, so that I might have sent you away with mirth and songs, with tambourines and lyre?" (Gen. 31:26–27).

In the Exodus narrative we have a form of the Hebrew verb which means "cause to go out," and the subject of this verb is always God or God acting through Moses. In this way (by his use of the causative form of the verb) the biblical narrator emphasizes that the people did not come out or gain their manumission through their own agency but solely through God. As Professor David Daube says: "The public is to be made conscious by constant reminders, that their fathers did not merely 'go out' but that God 'brought them out': hence the narrators were not content with the simple form, they introduced the causative and indeed favoured it."[1] In this way God himself appears as the recoverer or redeemer of Israel, and the concept of redemption enters biblical history.

Say therefore to the people of Israel, "I am the Lord, and I will bring you out from under the burdens of the Egyptians, and I will deliver you from their bondage, and I will redeem you with an outstretched arm and with great acts of judgment" (Ex. 6:6).

But redemption by a relative or friend meant that the slave changed his master from the foreign lord to the relative or friend who redeemed him. He came under a certain obligation—albeit loving obligation—to this relative. So the Israelites after their redemption regarded themselves as especially God's people, his property, and realized that they had a special obligation to "serve" him. "Serve" is the same word as worship. This idea of obligation to the redeemer is seen in the verse following the one quoted above.

. . . and I will take you for my people, and I will be your God;

---

[1] David Daube, *The Exodus Pattern in the Bible* (Faber and Faber, London, 1963), p. 33, used with permission.

and you shall know that I am the Lord your God, who brought you out from under the burdens of the Egyptians (Ex. 6:7).

The Hebrews' formal submission to their new master, God, was made on Mount Sinai when they received the commandments and agreed to the laws which their new king imposed on them and when they organized his worship (as we shall see) with cultural equipment and practices similar to those which obtained for earthly kings and masters in Egypt and elsewhere.

Now let us look at the credentials of the representative whom God chose to go on his behalf to redeem the people.

FURTHER READING

Daube, David, *The Exodus Pattern in the Bible*. Faber and Faber, London, 1963. Most of the material for this chapter has been based on this book.

5 The Background of Moses

The story of a slave child hidden in a cradle made of bulrushes and then discovered and adopted by a princess while she and her maids were bathing in the Nile sounds like a picturesque fairy tale. Yet when one looks into the background of Egypt and the culture of the times, Moses' infancy, boyhood, and general background seem not to be a fairy tale but a distinct mark of the providence of God and an important part in his plan of salvation history. The present writer will try to sketch a probable background to the early life of Moses and to discover in it the reasonableness of the selection of this man by God for his special work. The background can, of course, be *only* probable, but if it can place the story of Moses in a more historical and contemporary setting, then the writer's purpose is fulfilled.

MOSES' LIFE IN EGYPT

Moses' career is probably dated around the thirteenth century B.C., during the long reign of Rameses II (*circa* 1290-1224 B.C.). It was Rameses who built the two cities mentioned in Exodus 1:11, Pithom and Rameses, on which the Israelites labored.

The Israelites must have reached the land of Canaan by

about 1250 B.C. because the Stele of Merneptah (1230 B.C.) says,[1]

> Israel is laid waste, its seed is not,
> Hurru [Palestine] is become a widow for Egypt.

Was it possible for a Hebrew child to be adopted by an Egyptian princess? We must not think in terms of our Western culture but in terms of a polygamous society. Pharaoh's daughter might well have been his wife for, since inheritance passed through the female line, the Pharaohs contracted marriages with not only their sisters but their daughters. It does not necessarily mean that the marriage was frequently consummated. The wealthy Egyptian men, especially the Pharaohs, would take both many wives and many concubines. Today, in the Middle East, one famous Muslim sheikh has thirty-nine wives and over three hundred children; he cannot remember precisely how many daughters he has.

This gives us a picture of the kind of life an Egyptian princess of that period might lead. She might live in one of the great harems of which archaeological sites have been discovered in Thebes, Memphis, and on the delta known as the land of Goshen, where the Israelites lived. Her companions might include not only other Egyptian ladies from the nobility but also slaves who were concubines. Numerous wives led to less pregnancies for each woman, and there may have been some women without children. It would not be absolutely impossible, then, for the "daughter of Pharaoh"

---

[1] James P. Pritchard, ed., *The Ancient Near East: An Anthology of Texts and Pictures* (Princeton University Press, Princeton, 1958), p. 231, used with permission. This is a commemorative hymn relating to Merneptah's victory over the Libyans.

to see a child and wish to adopt it and for the mother of Moses to come to nurse it in the palace. However, we must allow for some "poetic licence" in the biblical writers. It has been suggested that the princess who adopted Moses was Hatshepsut, the chief queen of Thutmosis II; she acted as regent for Thutmosis III when his father died in 1504 B.C. Hatshepsut had herself crowned king and proved able and ambitious, especially in organizing building programs and military campaigns. However, the sixteenth century B.C. would seem to be too early a date for the birth of Moses.

Once in the harem the child would join the innumerable other children; most probably the boys would be separated from the girls, and thus Moses would have followed the education of all the boys; possibly no one would have inquired about his lineage. Perhaps a number of foreign boys found themselves in this large household and were able to take advantage of the good education offered. We must not think of every Hebrew as being in exactly the same situation during the period of Jewish slavery in Egypt. Some might rise to power, and others be in abject slavery. Perhaps some retained little appreciation of their birth and origin.

A boy in one of the harems would receive a reasonable education. He would be taught to read and write and especially to prepare diplomatic and secretarial correspondence like the Tel El-Amarna letters.[2] He would be given athletic training, probably from a retired officer, and would be trained in military techniques. Probably he would gain knowledge of the geography of the country, and if this were

[2] These are documents which were discovered in 1887 by an Egyptian peasant woman in Middle Egypt. They are mainly documents belonging to the royal archives of Amenhotep III and his son (fourteenth century B.C.). The letters comprise correspondence between Egypt, Palestine, Syria, and Phoenicia.

the case, it might explain why Moses was able to lead the children of Israel safely across the Red Sea and the peninsula of Sinai.

When the boy or young man was trained, he would take up a position as a military officer, or as a priest or attendant in a temple, or as a diplomat or secretary, or as an administrator of Pharaoh's property, or as an overseer of a building project. The latter might explain why Moses was found walking around the building site and took it into his hands to punish the harsh Egyptian overseer.

If such were the educational background of Moses, it is reasonably easy to see why he was so well prepared to undertake his great task for God and Israel. Perhaps Aaron had similar training. Or perhaps he was a priest and that was why Moses put him in charge of the Israelite worship when he organized the cult on Sinai (Ex. 28).

Moses' career in Egypt was cut short, as we learn from Exodus 2:11–15, when, after he had killed an Egyptian overseer, the Pharaoh sought to kill him. Moses fled to Midian which is east of the Sinai peninsula, south of Edom on the borders of the Arabian desert. After a kindly act of delivering some young women from some obstructing shepherds and then helping them to draw water, Moses was invited to the house of a man called Reuel (or Jethro). Eventually he married one of Reuel's daughters, Zipporah. The stay of Moses in Midian may well have been providential for him. The Midianites were descendants of Abraham through his concubine Keturah, and it may well have been here that Moses came in contact with the religion of his forefathers: we cannot be sure that he would have known about this from the Egyptian court. Moses, as well as learning about the religion of Abraham, may well have had time for prayer and reflection while he shepherded his father-in-law's flocks. This may have been a relief from the paganism and probably from the wealth and luxury of Egypt.

MOSES' CALL FROM GOD

It was while Moses was tending the flock of Jethro that God appeared to him in the burning bush (Ex. 3:1–3; *compare* Acts 7:30). This phenomenon may have been the phenomenon known as St. Elmo's fire. Whether it was a natural or a miraculous phenomenon, God used it as a vehicle of revelation to Moses and sent him on the mission to rescue Israel from its bondage. Moses was the representative whom God chose and, as such, it was necessary for him to know who was sending him and to have credentials to show those to whom he was sent. God supplied him with both of these. God partially revealed his name and nature to Moses.

Then Moses said to God, "If I come to the people of Israel and say to them 'The God of your fathers has sent me to you,' and they ask me, 'What is his name?' what shall I say to them?" God said to Moses, "I am who I am." And he said, "Say this to the people of Israel, 'I am has sent me to you.' . . . this is my name for ever, and thus I am to be remembered throughout all generations" (Ex. 3:13–15).

We cannot know precisely what was revealed to Moses at this moment, but it is not outside the bounds of possibility that Moses gained a profound idea or philosophical conception of God's nature indicated by the name "I am who I am," that is, I am unknowable, or pure essence, or he who is always with you. Further, this revelation might have been the culminating development of a concept which Moses had first learned in Egypt, namely, the concept of one supreme god, a concept which for a time, but not very successfully, was promulgated by Amenhotep IV, who saw the god of the sun-disk, Aton, as the supreme being and began a cult of monolatry (that is, worship, not necessarily belief, in one god). The revelation which Moses received on Mount Sinai in the burning bush may have been supernatural knowledge added to natural reasoning. Certainly, Moses must have been a man of high intelligence.

The other credential which Moses received was the power to perform signs and wonders. God showed him two of these: first, the making of the rod into a serpent (Ex. 4:1–5), and second, the fact that his arm became leprous and then was miraculously cleansed (Ex. 4:6–7). God also told him that he would be able to make the water of the Nile like blood (Ex. 4:9).

Moses was commissioned like a prophet (*compare* Is. 6, Jer. 1, and St. Paul in Acts 9:3–6) and, like a prophet, Moses out of humility declined the mission. He complained that he was not eloquent. God gave him Aaron as a spokesman: we need not, however, believe that this indicates that Moses had a speech impediment; he appears to have been quite eloquent later on in his career. It was probably considered fitting for one whom God called to confess his unworthiness in this fashion. So Moses was called and "sent" like one on a mission. Yet, without denying the supernatural elements and influence in Moses' life, we can without temerity suggest that as well as receiving a call from God, Moses also received intelligence from Egypt that the Pharaoh who sought his life was dead. Moses had fled from Egypt along the route taken by many runaway slaves, and it is not improbable that from time to time he may have received news about conditions in Egypt. Perhaps Aaron himself kept him informed and told him when the road was safe, for Aaron went out to meet Moses.

The Lord said to Aaron, "Go into the wilderness to meet Moses." So he went and met him at the mountain of God and kissed him. And Moses told Aaron all the words of the Lord with which he had sent him, and all the signs which he had charged him to do (Ex. 4:27–28).

It may have been a providential meeting inspired by God but it need not have been miraculous.

MOSES AND PHARAOH

Aaron and Moses went before Pharaoh to request that the Israelites should be allowed to go out into the wilderness for three days to worship their God. To us nowadays this may appear to be a strange request from slaves who were treated with oppression and cruelty. However, if we look at historical documents of Egypt, we find that there is evidence of workmen taking a leave of absence; the documents record the names of the absentees and the reasons why they were absent. One journal of absences takes note in several places of a workman "offering to his god"; the word "idle" is often noted (*compare* Ex. 5:8). Therefore, this request was not unusual.

But Pharaoh did not allow them to go; so Moses began to show his credentials to Pharaoh. The culmination of his display of credentials (or the judgments of God) were the ten plagues. All of these are natural occurrences in Egypt. The Nile becomes dull red about the time of August because of numerous tiny organisms in it; sometimes there are plagues of frogs about September; dead frogs might well give rise to lice and flies, and these in turn can cause pestilence among the cattle. Hail is rare in Egypt but it has been known. Locust plagues are known even today, and still in the East "locust forecasts" are broadcast over the radio when a cloud of locusts is seen approaching, in order to enable the farmers to prepare insecticides. Thick darkness may be explained by the sand storms which are brought about by the Khamsin, the hot desert wind, which occurs in the Egyptian spring. This usually lasts about two to four days; in Exodus 10:22 we read that the thick darkness lasted three days.

The plagues, then, in themselves are "signs" rather than miracles. The Hebrews distinguished between them by seeing a "sign" as a phenomenon, which could be explained naturally but whose timing might be providential, and by understanding "miracles" as due to God's direct intervention which was inexplicable by man. The providential element in the plagues lay in their severity and the fact that they appeared relatively close together, that is, in the same year. We need not think of the plagues as following one after the other punctiliously. It was the continuance of the plagues and the fear induced by them that made Pharaoh at long last urge the children of Israel to go.

The last plague was the one which tipped the balance. The first-born of the Egyptians, both cattle and men, were struck dead. God was obliged to go to the length of the *lex talionis* treatment in Exodus 4:23. This scene is dramatized in a sermon by Bishop Melito of Sardis in the second century of the Christian era:

. . . Egypt, the enemy, the unbelieving one. In one night he smote her and made her childless. For when the angel had gone about Israel and had seen him sealed with the blood of the sheep, he went forth against Egypt, and subdued the stiff-necked Pharaoh with grief, clothing him not with a robe of mourning nor with rent mantle, but with all Egypt, in rent garments, mourning for her first-born. For all Egypt, in sorrow and distress, with tears and beating of the breast, came to Pharaoh all in mourning, not only in the body but also in the soul, having rent not only robes . . . but also the breasts of her wantonness. There was a strange sight to see, here men beating their breasts, there wailing, and in the midst Pharaoh sitting mourning in sackcloth and ashes, and clothed with palpable darkness as with a cloak of mourning, girt with all Egypt as with a garment of endless grief. . . . These were the troubles which encompassed the Egyptians: a long night, palpable darkness, groping Death, a destroying angel, and Hades swallowing up their first-born. . . . In the darkness that could be felt was hidden death that could not be felt, and the unhappy Egyptians were groping in the darkness, while Death was groping and seeking out the first-born sons of the Egyptians. . . . the long silence of death came upon him [the first-born], saying, I am first-born Law; I am thy destiny, the silence of death. . . .

Perhaps Melito was not inaccurate in describing the great fear and catastrophe of that night when the God of Israel redeemed his people.

FURTHER READING

Cottrell, Leonard, *Life Under the Pharaohs.* Holt, New York, 1960.

Nims, Charles F., and Swaan, Wim, *Thebes of the Pharaohs.* Stein and Day, New York, 1965.

Pfeiffer, Charles F., *Egypt and the Exodus.* Baker Books, Grand Rapids, Mich., 1964.

6 The Passover

Before the Israelites set out from Egypt, Moses arranged that they should reenact an old shepherd festival which may even have been practiced by Abraham; similar ceremonies are still found among the Bedouin nomads today.

The shepherds of old used to perform a special ceremony as they passed from one grazing pasture to another; this usually occurred in the springtime. They would take an animal from their flocks and sacrifice it and then daub the blood of the animal on the tentpoles of their dwellings. This ceremony was what we call an apotropaic ceremony, that is, a ceremony to scare away or propitiate evil powers so that they did not harm the new flock. The shepherds then ate the roasted animal and with it the bitter herbs which are found in the desert. The whole ceremony apparently took place at the full moon, which would provide light for the participants.

Moses may have learnt about this ceremony when he lived as a shepherd in Midian with his father-in-law's flock. At "the going out" of the children of Israel from Egypt, however, he raised it to a feast of incomparably greater, indeed perpetual, importance. It was set in the historical event of the emigration from Egypt when the people passed, not from one grass pasture to another, but from slavery to freedom and from abject living to a land flowing with milk and honey.

53

THREE PASSOVER ACCOUNTS

In Exodus 12 we seem to have at least three accounts of the same institution of the shepherd festival which is now called the Passover. At this point we will show how the Pentateuch (first five books of the bible) is composed. The Pentateuch is a collection of materials gathered from various sources and traditions. One of these we call the J strand, J standing for Jahweh because the name used for God is Jahweh (or Yahweh), which originated about 950–850 B.C. Then there is a strand called E, which stands for Elohim, because the name used for God in this collection of material is usually Elohim; this had its origin around 850–750 B.C. Third, we have a strand called P, the Priestly strand, named thus because P shows an interest in priestly details, such as sacrifices and levitical cleanliness; P arose about 638–450 B.C. There is another strand, D (Deuteronomy), but this only concerns the book of Deuteronomy and some of Joshua. When the biblical compiler composed his writings, he often placed the material as told by the different strands side by side; sometimes he might have interwoven them. This explains why at times we find inconsistencies and repetitions in the bible.

If we turn to Exodus 12 we find approximately the following arrangement:

verses 1–13 is the Priestly strand;
verses 14–20 the Priestly strand (about the Feast of Unleavened Cakes, not the Passover);
verses 21–27 Jahweh strand;
verse 28 Priestly strand;
verses 29–32 Jahweh strand (death of the first-born of Egypt);

verses 33–34 Jahweh strand;
verses 35–36 Elohim strand.

If we examine the earliest strand, that is, the Jahweh strand, we see that the account of the Passover ceremony in Egypt is very close to the shepherd festival. Verses 21–28 describe Moses calling together the elders of the people in a kind of ad hoc manner and telling them to select lambs for their families and then to slaughter the lambs. Then the apotropaic ceremony is demanded. The blood of the lamb is sprinkled on the doorposts and lintels of the Israelite houses, not now to protect the animals but to protect the people from the plague which will strike the first-born of the Egyptians. The people (*v.* 22) are forbidden to go out in the night, probably because of the ancient belief that the darkness is full of evil spirits. They are told that

. . . the Lord will pass through to slay the Egyptians; and when he sees the blood on the lintel and on the two doorposts, the Lord will pass over the door, and will not allow the destroyer to enter the houses to slay you (Ex. 12:23).

The mention of the "destroyer" betrays the early character of this portion of the text; the "destroyer" is equivalent to the evil spirit which attacked the flocks of the nomads. The next portion of the Jahweh strand, verses 29–32, describes the death of the first-born in Egypt; it is dramatic in its simplicity. Then, the people of Israel dash away, taking their dough and their kneading bowls with them.[1]

When we turn to the Priestly strand we find that it con-

---

[1] Concerning these ceremonies, *compare* G. E. Mendenhall, "Puppy and Lettuce in Northwest-semitic Covenant Making," *Bulletin of American Society for Oriental Research* 133 (1954), pp. 26–30.

tains many details which are not applicable to the historical
occasion of the Exodus. First of all, in verses 3–6 we read
that the people are to select their animals on the tenth day
of the month and that these lambs must be without blemish,
male, a year old; and then they are to slay the lambs on the
fourteenth day in the evening before the whole assembly of
Israel. This presupposes that the festival can be planned with
perfection and also that all the people can gather together:
it is unlikely that they did this in Egypt. The apotropaic
ceremony is still performed, but there are special details
about the cooking of the lamb.

Do not eat any of it raw or boiled with water, but roasted, its
head with its legs and its inner parts. And you shall let none of it
remain until the morning, anything that remains until the morning you shall burn (Ex. 12:9–10).

The last verse shows that the meal has taken on a sacred
character; none must be left in case it might be desecrated.
Further, we notice that it must be eaten with unleavened
bread and bitter herbs. The use of bitter herbs may have
originated in the shepherd festival; the required use of
unleavened bread during the meal may have been an
addition to the Passover at the time it became combined
with a harvest festival.

Verses 14–20 add priestly regulations about the feast;
again, there are details which could not have been observed
in the land of Egypt. They include the eating of unleavened
bread for seven days, with a holy assembly on the first and
the seventh days on which no work can be done: if anyone
eats what is leavened he shall be cut off from the community.

It might be interesting to take one more text concerning
the feast of the Passover to show further developments or

changes in the conduct of the feast. If we take Deuteronomy 16:1–8, we find that the Passover is no longer a home festival, conducted by a family or groups of families. It is a national festival and must be performed only in one place (probably Jerusalem).

You may not offer the passover sacrifice within any of your towns which the Lord your God gives you; but at the place which the Lord your God will choose, to make his name dwell in it, there you shall offer the passover sacrifice, in the evening at the going down of the sun, at the time you came out of Egypt (Deut. 16:5–6).

Further, the victim is no longer roasted but boiled (*v.* 7). Thus, the Passover developed from a simple shepherd feast to a festival commemorative of a great historical event and was focused entirely around the national metropolis.

These texts show the evolution of religious ideas and a religious ceremony; this same methodology can be applied to other ideas and feasts in the bible. Nowadays, the Passover among the Jews is a home festival once again and one of joy, a feast during which they narrate all the benefits of the Savior who brought them out of Egypt and when they look forward again to complete freedom; this they have already realized at least politically since 1947 in the land of Israel. The central idea in this feast is the theme that God and no one else brought them out of Egypt; he was their sole redeemer. One of the oldest passages in the Jewish Passover service reads,

. . . And the Lord brought us out of Egypt—not by the hand of an angel, and not by the hand of a seraph, and not by the hand of a messenger, but by the Holy One, blessed be He, in His

glory and in His person, as it is said: "For I will go through the land of Egypt in that night, and I will smite all the first-born in the land of Egypt. . . . I, not an angel. . . . I, not a seraph. . . . I, not a messenger. I *am* the Lord—I am He, and no other . . ."

We shall note later in the book the importance of the Passover for the Christian Eucharist, the new covenant in Christ's blood.

FURTHER READING

Gaster, T. H., *Passover: Its History and Traditions*. Beacon, Boston, 1962 (paperback).

Segal, J. B., *The Hebrew Passover from the Earliest Times to* A.D. 70. Oxford University Press, New York, 1963.

De Vaux, R., *Studies in Old Testament Sacrifice*. University of Wales Press, Cardiff, 1964.

7 The Covenant on Mount Sinai

Moses, Aaron, and the children of Israel escaped from Egypt.[1] We will not discuss their route in the wilderness, the knowledge of which is still very uncertain, and will pass directly to a consideration of the covenant on Mount Sinai. This is recorded in Exodus 19 and 20; another account is given in Exodus 34, but we will concentrate on the first account.

THE COVENANT AND THE COMMANDMENTS

The people were encamped in the wilderness of Sinai (Ex. 19). Moses ascended the mountain and received a revelation from God to this effect:

Thus you shall say to the house of Jacob, and tell the people of Israel: You have seen what I did to the Egyptians, and how I bore you on eagles' wings and brought you to myself. Now therefore, if you will obey my voice and keep my covenant, you shall be my own possession among all peoples; for all the earth is mine, and you shall be to me a kingdom of priests and a holy nation. These are the words which you shall speak to the children of Israel (Ex. 19:3–6).

---

[1] There may, of course, have been more than one emigration from Egypt, with small groups escaping at various times.

In these words God reaffirmed the promise and covenant which he had made with Abraham in Genesis 12, 15, and 17. Moses called the people and bade them purify themselves in preparation for renewing the covenant and witnessing God's affirmation of this renewal.

And the Lord said to Moses, "Go to the people and consecrate them today and tomorrow, and let them wash their garments, and be ready by the third day; for on the third day the Lord will come down upon Mount Sinai in the sight of all the people" (Ex. 19:10–11).

The Lord signified his Presence by a kind of volcanic eruption of the mountain, and the people kept at a distance; but Moses and Aaron were bidden to ascend to the Lord. Then God delivered the ten commandments, which are known as the decalogue (Ex. 20:1–17).

The biblical account does not tell us exactly what happened—how Moses received the ten commandments—but it tries to convey to us what they meant to him and the people. The children of Israel had escaped from the tyranny of the Pharaoh and they knew that God had redeemed them. We have said that a slave who was redeemed owed a certain obligation and submission to his redeemer. It is in the ten commandments that we see the people of Israel formally and solemnly renouncing their allegiance to Pharaoh and the religion of Egypt (which was intimately bound up with politics)and accepting God as their king.

Recent research has shown that Moses with his genius used for his solemn contract of the people with God the cultural media of the day. Many scholars would think that the ten commandments and certain other obligations imposed on the Israelites bear close affinity to the stipulations

in Hittite treaties with contemporary Egypt. In the reign of
Rameses, before the children of Israel had escaped, a treaty
had been made between Egypt and the Hittites.[2] Moses may
have used a similar format to express the treaty or covenant
between God and Israel.

THE DECALOGUE AND THE
HITTITE TREATIES

We shall now examine the ten commandments and ger-
mane texts in the Old Testament to find their affinity with
Hittite treaties. Then we shall look at what is known as the
Book of the Covenant (Ex. 20:18–23:22) and certain other
texts to show their affinity with such laws as the Code of
Hammurabi, which was probably drawn up by a Babylonian
king of the eighteenth century B.C. We shall see some similarity between biblical material and nonbiblical legal and
cultural texts which makes us realize the historicity of the
biblical narratives.

1. A Hittite treaty began with a preamble giving the name
of the "great king"; for example,

Treaty of Rea-machesha mai Amena, the great king, the king of
the land of Egypt, the valiant, with Hatusilis, the great king of
the Hatti land . . . (*compare* Ex. 20:1, "I am the Lord your God").

Then the treaty gave a prologue which related the beneficial
deeds of the king. This took the form of a dialogue between

[2] The Hittites were an old nation; as an ethnic group they lived in
Canaan in the time of the patriarchs. They founded an empire about 1800
B.C. and something of the history of this has been discovered from archives
since 1906 A.D. Their empire reached its zenith about 1400 B.C. and col-
lapsed around 1200 B.C.

"I and thou"; *compare:*

I am the Lord your God, who brought you out of the land of Egypt, out of the house of bondage (Ex. 20:2; cf. Ex. 19:3–6 quoted above).

for establishing [good] peace [and] good brotherhood [worthy of] great [king] forever.[3]

2. After this the treaty imposed certain obligations which the subjects accepted. There were, for example, prohibitions about having foreign relations outside the Hittite Empire. In the same way Moses showed that God forbade allegiance or association not only with other gods but also with the people who worshiped these gods.

You shall have no other gods before me. You shall not make for yourself a graven image, or any likeness of anything that is in heaven above, or that is in the earth beneath, or that is in the water under the earth; you shall not bow down to them or serve them; for I the Lord your God am a jealous God (Ex. 20:3–5).

This commandment must have been arresting to a people who had just emigrated from a land which worshiped the vulture goddess of Nekheb; the serpent goddess of Buto; the fire goddess, Sekhmet of Memphis; the falcon god, Horus; Sobek, the crocodile god; Khum, the ram; Hathor, the cow; and also gods with human forms. It is no wonder that while the people were waiting for Moses to come down from the mountain they made and worshiped a golden calf, for they must have known the sacred animals of Egypt.

The most important of these animals was the Apis Bull

---

[3] James B. Pritchard, ed., *Ancient Near Eastern Texts Relating to the Old Testament,* rev. ed. (Princeton University Press, Princeton, 1955), p. 202.

which was black with white spots and with a white triangle on the forehead and the figure of a crescent moon on the right side.[4] These deceased bulls were given elaborate burials near Memphis. Rameses II laid out an elaborate gallery in which bulls were buried in stone sarcophagi. The gallery, known as the Serapeum, was carved out of solid rock. "It was three hundred fifty feet long with rows of niches for the burial of individual bulls. Many pious pilgrims came to the Serapeum to venerate the bulls as late as the Ptolemaic period."[5]

It is understandable, therefore, that the Israelites were bidden to have no association with foreign peoples; this was perhaps the only way in which Moses could wean the people from the paganism to which they had grown accustomed: it is not a wonder that the Israelites fell into idolatry but a wonder that they acquired so sophisticated a religion in such a short time. The following is one of the texts which deals with the expulsion of pagan peoples:

When my angel goes before you, and brings you in to the Amorites, and the Hittites, and the Perizzites, and the Canaanites, the Hivites, and the Jebusites, and I blot them out, . . . you shall utterly overthrow them and break their pillars in pieces. . . . And I will send hornets before you, which shall drive out Hivite, Canaanite, and Hittite from before you. . . . You shall make no covenant with them or with their gods. They shall not dwell in your land, lest they make you sin against me; for if you serve their gods, it will surely be a snare to you (Ex. 23:23–32).

This passage is contained in what is named the Book of the Covenant. At that stage of religious evolution radical exter-

[4] C. F. Pfeiffer, *Egypt and the Exodus* (Baker Books, Grand Rapids, Mich., 1964), p. 24.
[5] *Ibid.*

mination of pagan people was ordered so that their paganism might be obliterated.

3. Next, Hittite treaties required the subject peoples to fight for the king when required. The Israelites certainly regarded their warfare as a holy war for Yahweh, their God. For example, we can see this in the words of Deborah the prophetess.

She . . . summoned Barak . . . and said to him, "The Lord, the God of Israel, commands you, 'Go, gather your men at Mount Tabor, taking ten thousand from the tribe of Naphtali and the tribe of Zebulun. And I will draw out Sisera, the general of Jabin's army, to meet you by the river Kishon with his chariots and his troops; and I will give him into your hand' " (Judg. 4:6–7).

4. Further, the Hittite treaties required the vassals to bring tribute each year to the king, in whom they are to put complete trust. We can see a similar idea reflected in the Israelite practice of appearing three times a year before God, their king.

Three times in the year shall all your males appear before the Lord God (Ex. 23:17; *compare* also Deut. 26).

5. One other stipulation was made by the Hittite king, namely, that his vassals should submit disputes with other vassals to the adjudication of the king or his representative. We find a similar enactment for the Israelites.

If any case arises requiring decision between one kind of homicide and another, one kind of legal right and another, or one kind of assault and another, any case within your towns which is too difficult for you, then you shall arise and go up to the place which the Lord your God will choose, and coming to the Levitical priests, and to the judge who is in office in those days, you shall consult them, and they shall declare to you the decision. . . . you shall not turn aside from the verdict which they declare to you, either to the right hand or to the left (Deut. 17:8–11).

We also find Moses judging the people and selecting men to help him in this task in Exodus 18.

6. After these stipulations the treaty was deposited in the shrine of the god and was to be read in public at certain times. We find this kind of provision in Deuteronomy.

And Moses wrote this law and gave it to the priests . . . and to all the elders of Israel. And Moses commanded them, "At the end of every seven years, at the set time of the year of release, at the feast of booths, when all Israel comes to appear before the Lord your God at the place which he will choose, you shall read this law before all Israel in their hearing. Assemble the people, men, women, and little ones, and the sojourner within your towns, that they may hear and learn to fear the Lord your God, and be careful to do all the words of this law" (Deut. 31:9–12).

The law of the God of Israel was placed in the ark of the covenant (which we will explain later) instead of the shrine of the god. In a Hittite treaty the gods were called to be witnesses. In the case of Israel this detail was conspicuous by its absence; there were no other gods but Yahweh, and he himself came to seal the covenant (Ex. 19:16–24; 24; 34).

7. The treaty of the Hittites was normally concluded by a series of blessings and curses upon those who kept the treaty or broke it. Here are some blessings and curses from one Hittite treaty:

The words of the treaty and the oath that are inscribed on this tablet—should Duppi-Tessub not honor these words of the treaty and the oath, may these gods of the oath destroy Duppi-Tessub together with his person, his wife, his son, his grandson, his house, his land and together with everything that he owns.

We can compare these with the blessings and curses found in Deuteronomy 27 and 28, especially 27:15–26 and 28:1–6.

What was the precise meaning of this covenant on Mount Sinai? Primarily, it was a development of the covenant with Abraham, a fuller realization of it. The covenant with Abraham was simple. The only requirement on Abraham's side was male circumcision. But at the covenant on Mount Sinai, God's requirements were intended to pervade the whole life of the individual person and the whole community. God required total giving.

THE COVENANT AND THE HAMMURABI CODE

Israel's allegiance to Yahweh as king was no vague or sentimental relationship but involved the acceptance of detailed prescription concerning one's behavior toward God and toward his fellowmen. The Book of the Covenant, which is a type of commentary or detailed application of the ten commandments, is a concrete example of this. Israel was to have her moral and legal code just as the Hittites, for example, had theirs under Hammurabi. The Book of the Covenant is contained in Exodus 20:18–23:22.

It adds a touch of reality and historicity to the bible to see the correspondence between its legal codes and those of surrounding cultures. It is not known when the Israelites drew up the Book of the Covenant, but it must have been sometime after they had settled in Canaan, for many laws refer to agriculture; these laws would not have been applicable during the wanderings in the wilderness. Yet there is no mention of a king, so the Code is probably premonarchic, that is, before about 1050 B.C.

Outwardly the Book of the Covenant shows affinity to the Babylonian Code of Hammurabi (1800 B.C.), Assyrian laws (*circa* 1350 B.C.), and the Hittite Code (*circa* 1350 B.C.). The general law and then the exceptional case are found in all these codes. The main divisions of the Book of the Covenant follow those of the Code of Hammurabi, that is, it has laws of property and laws of persons. The laws of procedure are missing in the Book of the Covenant but are preserved in Deuteronomy 19:16–20. The details are interesting to compare. Let us look at some examples.

BOOK OF THE COVENANT	CODE OF HAMMURABI
1. You shall not utter a false report. You shall not join hands with a wicked man, to be a malicious witness. You shall not follow a multitude to do evil; nor shall you bear witness in a suit, turning aside after a multitude, so as to pervert justice; nor shall you be partial to a poor man in his suit (Ex. 23:1–3; *compare* also Deut. 5:20; 19:16-21).	If a seignior came forward with false testimony in a case, and has not proved the word which he spoke, if that case was a case involving life, that seignior shall be put to death (p. 139, no. 3).[6]
2. If a man steals an ox or a sheep, and kills it or sells it, he	If a seignior stole either an ox or a sheep or an ass or a pig or a

[6] All quotations from the Code of Hammurabi are taken from *The Ancient Near East: An Anthology of Texts and Pictures,* ed. by James B. Pritchard (Princeton University Press, Princeton, 1958, paperback), used with permission.

shall pay five oxen for an ox, and four sheep for a sheep. He shall make restitution; if he has nothing, then he shall be sold for his theft. If the stolen beast is found alive in his possession, whether it is an ox or an ass or a sheep, he shall pay double (Ex. 22:1–4).

3. When you buy a Hebrew slave, he shall serve six years, and in the seventh he shall go out free, for nothing. If he comes in single, he shall go out single; if he comes in married, then his wife shall go out with him. If his master gives him a wife and she bears him sons or daughters, the wife and her children shall be her master's and he shall go out alone (Ex. 21:2–4).

4. If a man delivers to his neighbour money or goods to keep, and it is stolen out of the man's house, then, if the thief is found, he shall pay double (Ex. 22:7).

5. When men strive together, and hurt a woman with child, so that there is a miscarriage, and yet no harm follows, the one who hurt her shall be fined, according as the woman's husband shall lay

goat, if it belonged to the church [or] if it belonged to the state, he shall make thirtyfold restitution; if it belonged to a private citizen, he shall make good tenfold. If the thief does not have sufficient to make restitution, he shall be put to death (p. 140, no. 8).

If an obligation came due against a seignior and he sold [the services of] his wife, his son, or his daughter, or he has been bound over to service, they shall work [in] the house of their purchaser or obligee for three years, with their freedom reestablished in the fourth year (p. 151, no. 117).

If a seignior gave silver, gold or any sort of thing for safe-keeping to a [nother] seignior in the presence of witnesses and he has denied [the fact] to him, they shall prove it against that seignior and he shall pay double whatever he denied (p. 151, no. 124).

If a seignior struck a [nother] seignior's daughter and has caused her to have a miscarriage, he shall pay ten shekels of silver for her fetus. If that woman has died, they shall put his daughter upon him; and he shall pay as the judges determine. If any harm follows, then you shall give life for life, eye for eye, tooth for tooth, hand for hand, foot for foot, burn for burn, wound for wound, stripe for stripe (Ex. 21:22–25).

to death. If by a blow he has caused a commoner's daughter to have a miscarriage, he shall pay five shekels of silver. If that woman has died, he shall pay one-half mina of silver. If he struck a seignior's female slave and has caused her to have a miscarriage, he shall pay two shekels of silver (p. 162, nos. 209-213).

From these examples it is evident that the biblical laws do show affinity to laws in other cultures of the same period. But when we look at the biblical laws, it is important to realize that they are incorporated into the making of the covenant[7] on the basis of the idea that all the divine legal requirements made of Israel have their root in the covenant relationship between God and the people. This fact is thrown into higher relief because the laws end with Yahweh's assurance of success and blessing on Israel if they are obeyed.

Behold, I send an angel before you, to guard you on the way and to bring you to the place which I have prepared. Give heed to him and hearken to his voice, do not rebel against him, for he will not pardon your transgression; for my name is in him. But if you harken attentively to his voice and do all that I say, then I will be an enemy to your enemies and an adversary to your adversaries (Ex. 23:20–22).

The God of Abraham was accepted at Sinai as God and king, and the ethical requirements of the community and nation were seen to emanate from him. One last thing was left: the establishment of the official worship of God.

---

[7] The laws may be later, but the fact that the compiler(s) of the Pentateuch placed them in the Sinai tradition is of theological importance.

THE KINGLY COURT

Worship in the age of the patriarchs was very simple, in keeping with their seminomad existence. They established places of worship where God had appeared to them or where they had received a message from God. Thus, Abraham's first halt in the land of Canaan was at Shechem, at the place where the Oak of Moreh stood (probably, a Canaanite sanctuary), and

Then the Lord appeared to Abram, and said, "To your descendants I will give this land." So he built there an altar to the Lord, who had appeared to him (Gen. 12:7).

Similarly, Jacob experienced a theophany (appearance of God) at Bethel. It is an arresting scene and one which may have influenced John 1:51.

And he [Jacob] dreamed that there was a ladder set up on the earth, and the top of it reached to heaven; and behold, the angels of God were ascending and descending on it! And behold, the Lord stood above it and said, "I am the Lord, the God of Abraham your father and the God of Isaac; the land on which you lie I will give to you and to your descendants; and your descendants shall be like the dust of the earth, and you shall spread abroad to the west and to the east and to the north and to the south; and by you and your descendants shall all the families of the earth bless themselves. Behold, I am with you and will keep you wherever you go, and will bring you back to this land; for I will not leave you until I have done that of which I have spoken to you." Then Jacob awoke from his sleep and said, "Surely the Lord is in this place; and I did not know it." And he was afraid, and said, "How awesome is this place! This is none other than the house of God, and this is the gate of heaven" (Gen. 28:12–17).

The patriarchs did not have as firm a monotheistic belief as probably did the Israelites from about the time of Moses. They may well have used pagan shrines. Some appear to have had other gods in their houses; for example, Jacob says to his household,

Put away the foreign gods that are among you, and purify yourselves, and change your garments (Gen. 35:2).

In the desert the people learned that they formed an individual nation with an individual God. They also firmly believed the promise of God to Abraham, namely, that Canaan was the land which God had given them. They set off to conquer that land and to establish the true religion. They were not unlike crusaders engaged in a holy war.

Connected with this idea is the furniture which they used in their cult (worship). The central feature was the ark. This was a chest of acacia wood with gold plates; rings were attached to it, with poles passed through the rings in order that the chest might be carried. Over the ark was placed a plate of gold, the same size as the ark, called the *kapporet,* the propitiatory or mercy seat; two cherubim guarded this with their wings.[8] The ark symbolized the empty throne of God. It was constructed like the ancient thrones of the pagan gods, which were frequently in the form of chests; but it had no image of God on it. The ark was carried into battle.

And whenever the ark set out, Moses said, "Arise, O Lord, and let thy enemies be scattered; and let them that hate thee flee before thee." And when it rested, he said, "Return, O Lord, to the ten thousand thousands of Israel" (Num. 10:35–36).

[8] The mercy seat may have been a later addition to the ark of the covenant.

The ark was a realistic symbol of the presence of Yahweh, and it was the medium through which the deity led his people in their wanderings and in war. It was a great catastrophe when it was captured by the enemy (see 1 Sam. 4:17).

The Israelites, led by Moses and Aaron, used the tent shrine in their worship of God. The tent or tabernacle is to be thought of in connection with the ark, but it was not eclipsed by the ark. It may have been a mere covering for the ark. On the other hand, it may have been a shrine in its own right. It, too, was a nomad war apparatus. The description of the tabernacle is found in Exodus 26; although this is a late account from the Priestly source and is somewhat exaggerated, we can understand the general idea of the structure.

The tabernacle was a rectangular building with a wooden frame. It was open on the eastern side and covered with finely woven material embroidered with figures or cherubim. Over this material was stretched a layer of goat skin, "like a tent over the dwelling." Lastly, the whole structure was covered with ram skins dyed red and then with lighter leather hides (Ex. 26;36:8–38). There was a curtain over the entry to the structure, and a costly veil across the innermost part marked the division between the Holy Place and the Holy of Holies. Behind the veil was the ark and in the Holy Place were the candlestick and the table of shewbread. Around the dwelling was an open court edged with a barrier of bronze posts and silver curtain rods from which the linen curtains fell down to the ground (Ex. 27:9–19).

This tent or tabernacle was like the tents in use by the ancient (and also modern) Bedouin tribes. They had little tents or litters, and these were the last objects which they picked up when moving to a new pasture: they carried them on their camels. In battle the sheikh's daughter or another beautiful girl used to ride in one of the tents to spur on the fighting men. The tent was considered to have supernatural power. Archaeology confirms these ideas, for little statues from Syria have been found which represent women (goddesses or assistants in the cult) riding on a camel in a litter covered by a pavilion. A bas-relief from Palmyra of the first century A.D. shows a religious procession carrying a tent, and the relief still shows the red coloring of the tent.

Thus, Israel had nomad tents, and naturally one was built for Yahweh. The tent seems to have disappeared when they reached the land of Canaan. The last indisputable mention of it is found in Numbers 25:6 when the Israelites were in the plains of Moab, their last station before they entered the Promised Land.

What is the theological importance of the tent? It was the place where God descended periodically (represented by a cloud ascending and descending) to talk face to face with Moses, to grant the petitions presented to him by his subjects, to hold court, and to give judgment like an earthly king.

Now Moses used to take the tent and pitch it outside the camp, far off from the camp; and he called it the tent of meeting. And every one who sought the Lord would go out to the tent of meeting, which was outside the camp. Whenever Moses went out to the tent, all the people rose up, and every man stood at his tent door, and looked after Moses, until he had gone into the tent. When Moses entered the tent, the pillar of cloud would descend and stand at the door of the tent, and the Lord would speak with Moses. And when all the people saw the pillar of cloud standing at the door of the tent, all the people would rise up and worship, every man at his tent door. Thus the Lord used to speak to Moses face to face, as a man speaks to his friend.

When Moses turned again into the camp, his servant Joshua the son of Nun, a young man, did not depart from the tent (Ex. 33:7–11).

It was the transcendent God who manifested himself in the tent, but it was the immanent presence of God which was symbolized in the ark. The transcendent God came at particular times when he was especially needed to guide the internal affairs of the people, for example, through the giving of oracles. The ark and the tabernacle enabled the Hebrews to reconcile two seemingly irreconcilable theological points, namely, the transcendence and the immanence of God. The ark had a longer history than the tabernacle, and was placed eventually in Jerusalem. Finally the Temple superseded both these pieces of liturgical furniture, and God was held to dwell among his people in a special way in the Temple built by King Solomon (1 Kings 6).

Thus, the development of the liturgy among the Hebrews shows a development in their concept of the deity. The God of heaven and earth worshiped by Abraham is transformed into a king excluding all other monarchs over his people. He is seen partly as a War-God. After the conquest of the Promised Land he resides in his court, the Temple. The most remarkable aspect of all is that the Israelites never made an image of their God. Thousands of statues and figurines of pagan gods and goddesses have been found, but not one has been discovered portraying Yahweh.

We turn now to the men of God, the prophets, who strove to maintain the purity of the Israelite religion and the fidelity of the Israelites to the covenant of Mount Sinai and the obligations which they freely accepted from their king on the day when

... Moses came and called the elders of the people, and set before them all these words which the Lord had commanded him. And all the people answered together and said, "All that the Lord has spoken we will do." And Moses reported the words of the people to the Lord. And the Lord said to Moses, "Lo, I am coming to you in a thick cloud, that the people may hear when I speak with you, and may also believe you for ever" (Ex. 19:7–9).

FURTHER READING

Mendenhall, G. E., "Ancient Oriental and Biblical Law." *Biblical Archaeologist* 17 (1954), pp. 24-46. "Covenant Forms in Israelite Tradition." *Ibid.*, pp. 50–76.

Oesterreicher, John M., *The Israel of God*. Prentice-Hall, Englewood Cliffs, N. J., 1963.

Pfeiffer, C. F., *Egypt and Exodus*. Baker Books, Grand Rapids, Mich., 1964.

Pritchard, J. B., *Ancient Near Eastern Texts*. Princeton University Press, Princeton, 1955.

De Vaux, R., *Ancient Israel*. McGraw-Hill, New York, 1962, pp. 271-329.

8 The Prophets

Now that we have charted an evolution in theological ideas from Abraham's ancestors, through Abraham, to Moses, and seen a development in liturgical worship from the simple syncretistic worship through that of the patriarchs to the "royal" worship emanating from Moses' authority, let us look at the growth and refinement of the prophetic phenomenon.

DEVELOPMENT OF THE PROPHETIC PHENOMENON

First of all, prophets were not peculiar to the Semitic or Hebrew peoples but were found among other peoples as well. We know, for example, from the Amarna Letters[1] that the king was the chief priest and acted as the leader of prophetic companies or guilds. From the Ugaritic texts the sacral king appears to be the chief of the priests and the chief of the shepherds. In these texts some scholars have found evidence of prophetic ecstasy, dreams, and oracles; in the Phoenician cults we find similar practices. Therefore, we cannot be surprised when we find prophets in Israelite society.

The first person to be given the title of prophet in the

[1] See p. 46 above.

76

Old Testament was Abraham (Gen. 20:7): he was a prophet in his capacity as a man of God, who was on special, intimate, and influential terms with God.

Now then restore the man's wife; for he is a prophet, and he will pray for you, and you shall live. But if you do not restore her, know that you shall surely die, you, and all that are yours (Gen. 20:7).

Thus God speaks to Abimelech when he has abducted Sarah.

But the prototype of all prophets was Moses. He was a prophet because he had a special call from God and because he had a prophetic awareness of history, sometimes discerning events beforehand. As a prophet he was profoundly concerned about ethical and social issues and above all held resolutely to monotheism. He interceded like a prophet on behalf of the people of God. All these qualities[2] appeared later in the outstanding prophets, such as Amos, Hosea, Isaiah, and Jeremiah—and also Jesus.

But before we study these let us look into prophecy in its most primitive form. Traditions about early prophecy are preserved in the books of Samuel and Kings. Prophets (and probably prophetesses) seem to have been professional people who lived together in guilds with common dwelling houses.

And Elisha came again to Gilgal when there was a famine in the land. And as the sons of the prophets were sitting before him, he said to his servant, "Set on the great pot, and boil pottage for the sons of the prophets." One of them went out into the field to gather herbs, and found a wild vine and gathered from it his lap full of wild gourds, and came and cut them up into the pot

---

[2] Attributed to Moses by the biblical writers, although they give a rather glorified portrait of him.

of pottage, not knowing what they were. And they poured out for the men to eat. But while they were eating of the pottage, they cried out, "O man of God, there is death in the pot!" And they could not eat it. He said, "Then bring meal." And he threw it into the pot, and said, "Pour out for the men, that they may eat." And there was no harm in the pot (2 Kings 4:38–41).

This incident shows the prophet Elisha as a master of a prophetic group, living together with his disciples. At the same time, it shows his miraculous powers. It is worth quoting the next few verses to show the affinity between his miracles and the miracles of Jesus, which we shall study later.

A man came from Baal-shalishah, bringing the man of God bread of the first fruits, twenty loaves of barley, and fresh ears of grain in his sack. And Elisha said, "Give to the men, that they may eat." But his servant said, "How am I to set this before a hundred men?" So he repeated, "Give them to the men, that they may eat, for thus says the Lord, 'They shall eat and have some left.' " So he set it before them. And they ate, and had some left, according to the word of the Lord (2 Kings 4:42–44).

Thus, the prophets living a community life seem to have had a leader or father; for example, when Elijah was carried up in the fiery chariot, his disciple Elisha cried,

My father, my father! the chariots of Israel and its horsemen! (2 Kings 2:12).

This leader probably trained the members of the guild in ecstatic exercises and instructed them in matters pertaining to the cult and the religion of Yahweh. Members are spoken of as "sitting before their leader" as did the disciples before

the Jewish teachers contemporary with Jesus. The prophets
married and had families.

Now the wife of one of the sons of the prophets cried to Elisha,
"Your servant my husband is dead; and you know that your servant feared the Lord, but the creditor has come to take my two
children to be his slaves" (2 Kings 4:1).

Elisha multiplied the woman's stock of oil so that she could
sell it and pay her debts and she and her sons could live on
the surplus money.

The chief duty of these prophets seems to have been to
deliver oracles. In the eyes of the people the prophets' special
relationship to God qualified them to receive messages from
God. Therefore, not only the common people but also kings
and queens went to inquire of them about quite mundane
matters. Rebekah, the wife of Isaac, inquired of the Lord
about the fate of her twins.

The children struggled together within her; and she said, "If it is
thus, why do I live?" So she went to inquire of the Lord. And the
Lord said to her, "Two nations are in your womb, and two
peoples, born of you, shall be divided; the one shall be stronger
than the other, the elder shall serve the younger" (Gen.
25:22–23).

Jacob did supplant Esau and became superior to him. King
Jeroboam sent his wife to Ahijah to inquire about their son
who was ill (1 Kings 14:1–20).[3] The inquirers usually
brought payment with them; for example, Jeroboam's wife
brought to the prophet a jar of honey, ten loaves, and some

---

[3] *Compare* also 2 Kings 1–2 concerning Elijah and 2 Kings 3:11–20;
8:1–15 concerning Elisha.

cakes; and the servant of the king of Syria (2 Kings 8:7 ff.) took forty camel-loads of presents to Elisha.

The prophets seem to have been involved in the cult or liturgical worship and to have had some functions similar to priests. They probably wandered about in large groups,[4] gathered more recruits, and then settled down for some time at places like Gilgal (2 Kings 4:38), Bethel (2 Kings 2:3), or Samaria (2 Kings 2:1 and 4:38), where there were sanctuaries and/or political centers. They seem to have worked and prophesied as a body. They sometimes performed a kind of ritual procession (1 Sam. 10:5), usually at a sanctuary or similar place (*compare* Is. 30:29). They seem to have fallen into ecstasy, that is, a physical and psychological condition —sometimes induced by music, dancing, rhythm—very much akin to insanity but not, as far as one could see, brought on by crude methods, such as slashing their bodies, as did the prophets of Baal (1 Kings 18) in their contest with Elijah (*compare* 2 Kings 9:11; 1 Sam. 21:12 ff.). In this state they seem to have given answers from God and to have prophesied. Perhaps the best example is the occasion when Saul was told by Samuel that he would meet a band of such prophets.

". . . and there, as you come to the city, you will meet a band of prophets coming down from the high place with harp, tambourine, flute, and lyre before them, prophesying. Then the spirit of the Lord will come mightily upon you, and you shall prophesy with them and *be turned into another man.*" . . . When they came to Gibeah, behold, a band of prophets met him; and the spirit of God came mightily upon him, and he prophesied among them. And when all who knew him before saw how he prophesied with the prophets, the people said to one another, "What has come

---

[4] *Compare* Obadiah hiding a hundred prophets (1 Kings 18:3) and the four hundred prophets with King Ahab (1 Kings 22:6).

over the son of Kish? Is Saul also among the prophets?" (1 Sam. 10:5–6, 9–11).

The actions of these prophets is also illustrated in the incident where Saul, when king, sent messengers after David to take him.

Then Saul sent messengers to take David; and when they saw the company of the prophets prophesying, and Samuel standing as head over them, the Spirit of God came upon the messengers of Saul, and they also prophesied. When it was told Saul, he sent other messengers, and they also prophesied. And Saul sent messengers again the third time, and they also prophesied. Then he went himself to Ramah and came to the great well that is in Secu; and he asked, "Where are Samuel and David?" And one said, "Behold, they are at Naioth in Ramah." And he went from there to Naioth in Ramah; and the Spirit of God came upon him also, and as he went he prophesied, until he came to Naioth in Ramah. And he too stripped off his clothes, and he too, prophesied before Samuel, and lay naked all that day and all that night. Hence it is said, "Is Saul also among the prophets?" (1 Sam. 19:20–24).

This is a very arresting example of the contagious character of prophecy.[5] A phenomenon similar to this was Elijah's running before Ahab's chariot from Mount Carmel to Jezreel, certainly a feat of supernatural physical strength. Such prophets were also gifted with clairvoyance (2 Kings 8:7 ff.), thought reading, and telepathy, and some were also endowed with the gift of miracle working. Elisha performed the miracle of the widow's cruse (2 Kings 4), raised the dead (2 Kings 4), and cured leprosy (2 Kings 5). Even the clothes or staff of a prophet was thought to possess mirac-

[5] *Compare* also 1 Kings 22 where four hundred prophets fall into ecstacy.

ulous power, for example, Elijah's mantle (2 Kings 2:14) or Elisha's staff. These miracles are interesting as foreshadowing the miracles of Jesus and the apostles. We do not hear, however, of the prophets casting out demons. Perhaps the theology of demons had not developed among the Hebrews by that time.

REFINEMENT OF THE PROPHETIC PHENOMENON

Of most interest for theological development is the prophets' relationship to Yahweh, his covenant, and the peculiar destiny of the people of God, especially in keeping the religion of the Israelites free from idolatry and immorality. From the rather motley crew of prophets which we have glanced at in the pages of the Old Testament arose men of outstanding calibre who influenced the course of Israel's history and the development of her theology.

The prophets occupied a position which was part and parcel of Israelite politics. First of all, they were an integral part of the Israelite army. They were charismatic leaders and controlled the oracles, which were consulted before entering into war; they were connected with the shrines of Yahweh as War-God and probably to some extent had custody of the ark during wartime. During actual fighting they practiced war asceticism, warrior ecstasy—a collective ecstasy of the community or an individual ecstasy of the charismatic. This ecstasy was induced by war dances and perhaps by alcohol and orgies; this is probably behind the shouts upon the arrival of the ark.

When the ark of the covenant of the Lord came into the camp, all Israel gave a mighty shout, so that the earth resounded. And when the Philistines heard the noise of the shouting, they said,

"What does this great shouting in the camp of the Hebrews mean?" And when they learned that the ark of the Lord had come to the camp, the Philistines were afraid; for they said, "A god has come into the camp." And they said, "Woe to us! For nothing like this has happened before" (1 Sam 4:5–7).

Probably the Nazirites developed from these ecstatic warriors; the Nazirites consecrated themselves by growing their hair, not touching wine, and not approaching the dead (see Deut. 33:16 and the Song of Deborah in Judg. 4 and 5). These warriors were possibly tattooed on the forehead (*compare* 1 Kings 20:41), and the leaders of the schools probably threw coats over them (these may have been skins of animals offered in sacrifice and thought to have some supernatural power) as an outward sign of their office. The prophets in one capacity, therefore, appear as army chaplains and crusaders: this is understandable as all wars were religious ones at that time. The first liberation war was the Deborah War, and we can see her as the "mother of Israel," inciting her people to the crusade, promising victory, and winning it. Judges 5 is a liturgical victory song.

But as the composition of the army changed, the prophets became less important in this capacity. King Solomon imported horses and chariots and made an army of cavalry, and the ancient warrior ecstatics could not compete with the chariots; hence, they were demilitarized but still retained an important function in politics. They were still found at the court of the king and continued to influence his decisions about waging wars; the clearest example is that of Jehoshaphat, king of Judah, who asked the king of Israel to join him in battle.

And Jehoshaphat said to the king of Israel, "Inquire first for the word of the Lord." Then the king of Israel gathered four hundred men, and said to them, "Shall I go to battle against Ramoth-gilead, or shall I forbear?" And they said, "Go up; for the Lord will give it into the hand of the king." But Jehoshaphat said, "Is there not here another prophet of the Lord of whom we may inquire?" (1 Kings 22:5–7).

This chapter of First Kings is very informative with regard to the prophets. Their potent political influence as a professional body but not necessarily as individual sincere and true prophets is clearly evident. We see them exercising their function in a body, and in verse 11 we see an example of a prophetic *ôth*.[6]

And Zedekiah the son of Chenaanah made for himself horns of iron, and said, "Thus says the Lord, 'With these you shall push the Syrians until they are destroyed.' "

This was a dramatic symbolic action by the use of which the prophet believed he would affect the result of the forthcoming battle.

Then over against the band of prophets we see Micaiah, the true prophet of Yahweh, fearlessly telling the truth to the king of Judah. The criterion of true prophecy, as we see from verse 28, is whether what the prophet has foretold will come to pass. The events proved that Micaiah was a true prophet and the others were false.

Gradually the band of professional prophets seems to have lost its influence, and men of the stature of Micaiah rose to power feeling within themselves a special vocation from God to correct the king and his policies if they were not in accordance with the moral and religious standards of Yahweh.

---

[6] A prophetic *ôth* is an efficacious symbolic action or sign, which was believed to effect what it symbolized.

Hence, we find Elijah fulminating against the idolatry of Jezebel, King Ahab's wife, and against the injustice of Ahab in taking Naboth's vineyard (1 Kings 21).

In this way the prophets returned to some extent to the stature of Moses, as sincere men of God, not so much concerned with "magical" affairs and ecstasy; they were people who *forthtold* (that is, spoke publicly), rather than *foretold*. They became men of vision who realized that moral and religious degeneracy will bring upon the people the anger of God which brings in its wake political ruin, so they became champions of the decalogue and the Book of the Covenant given by God to the people of Israel. The criterion of a true prophet lay in his allegiance to the revelation of God on Mount Sinai, his acceptance of the authority of Moses, and his subscription to the doctrines of the Exodus event. The figures of Micaiah, Elijah, and Elisha developed into the classical prophets. Of these we shall study Amos and Hosea.

FURTHER READING

Haldar, A., *Associations of Cult Prophets among the Ancient Semites.* Almqvist and Wiksells, Uppsala, 1945.

Johnson, A. R., *The Cultic Prophets in Ancient Israel.* University of Wales Press, London, 1944.

Lindblom, J., *Prophecy in Ancient Israel.* Fortress, Philadelphia, 1962.

Rowley, H. H., "Ritual and Hebrew Prophets" in *Myth, Ritual and Kingship,* ed. by S. H. Hooke. Oxford University Press, New York, 1958.

9 The First Literary Man of God, Amos

Elijah, Elisha, Nathan,[1] and Micaiah are forerunners of the group of prophets who are traditionally called the "classical prophets." One important difference between the classical prophets and their antecedents is the fact that the prophecies of the former have been committed to writing, not necessarily by themselves or by another person or at one time; they seem to have been compiled over a period of time. The oracles and messages which they delivered were gathered together probably by their disciples and are preserved for us now in the Old Testament. Under these circumstances we are not always quite certain whether a prophetical book belongs entirely to one age and one person; therefore, the reader must use a discerning eye for differences in style and other details which could indicate composite authorship.

But for our present purpose we want to discover the prophet's relationship to and interest in the covenant of Yahweh. Therefore, our study will concentrate mainly upon this point. We shall consider only Amos and Hosea.

AMOS' BACKGROUND

Amos lived in the eighth century B.C. and came from the Southern Kingdom, that is, Judah. But he journeyed to the

[1] See 2 Sam. 7 and 12.

Northern Kingdom, Israel, to deliver his message. The political situation at the time was one of peace. King Uzziah (784–746) ruled in the Southern Kingdom, and King Jeroboam II (786–746) reigned in the Northern Kingdom, the land of Palestine having been divided into two after the death of Solomon in 930 B.C. The Northern Kingdom, Israel, was at the zenith of its power; Samaria, its capital, was proverbial for its prosperity and luxury, and the political powers surrounding it were fairly tranquil at the time.

Into this kingdom came Amos. He was a man of unknown parentage, but he originated from Tekoa, which most scholars would locate a few miles south of Jerusalem in the desert of Judah. Tekoa apparently was near the caravan routes, and some have suggested that it was a great Arab-Israelite literary center. If this were so, it would account for the magnificence of Amos' literary style and the width of his knowledge of people and countries which is evident from the nine chapters we possess.

Amos tells us (Amos 7:14) that his occupation was that of a shepherd and dresser of sycamore trees. A shepherd might easily engage in both occupations, and Amos seems to have been financially independent enough to give up his occupation and go on his mission for Yahweh. We cannot assert that Amos was a poor or uneducated shepherd or that he lived in the wilds of the country because he used rural images abundantly. He might have been a wealthy flock owner with hired servants under him, but it is unlikely that we shall ever know whether this was true or not.

From his short book we gather that Amos received visions from God (Chapters 7, 8, and the beginning of 9), and these may have constituted his call. The fact that they come toward the end of his book does not necessarily mean that they occurred late in his career.

He began heralding his message in Samaria, the capital of the Northern Kingdom, which was built by King Omri and was situated on the trade routes running through the rich plain of Esdraelon. King Ahab continued Samaria's building plans after Omri, and we hear of bazaars and streets owned by Syrians of Damascus and also of idolatrous temples and shrines. Thus, we catch a glance of a city becoming economically prosperous, but at the expense of the purity of its religious beliefs. Many prophets thought of Samaria as the center of idolatry and the symbol of defection from Yahweh.

After that Amos apparently moved to Bethel where there was an important sanctuary on an ancient site on which Abraham had worshiped. But Jeroboam I (*circa* 930 B.C.), in rivalry with Jerusalem, had converted it into a pagan shrine.

And Jeroboam said in his heart, "Now the kingdom will turn back to the house of David; if this people go up to offer sacrifices in the house of the Lord at Jerusalem, then the heart of this people will turn again to their lord, to Rehoboam king of Judah, and they will kill me and return to Rehoboam king of Judah." So the king took counsel, and made two calves of gold. And he said to the people, "You have gone up to Jerusalem long enough. Behold your gods, O Israel, who brought you up out of the land of Egypt." And he set one in Bethel, and the other he put in Dan. And this thing became a sin (1 Kings 12:26–30).

AMOS' MESSAGE

Jeroboam staffed the sanctuary at Bethel with his own priests and controlled the worship there. It was to this sanctuary that Amos went to deliver a message of condemnation against Israel. Amos prophesied that

Jeroboam shall die by the sword, and Israel must go into exile away from his land (Amos 7:11).

This was not pleasing to Amaziah, the high priest of the sanctuary, and he told Amos to return to his own country of the south. Amos retorted with an even more deadly prophecy against Amaziah himself.

Your wife shall be a harlot in the city, and your sons and your daughters shall fall by the sword, and your land shall be parceled out by line; you yourself shall die in an unclean land, and Israel shall surely go into exile away from its land (Amos 7:17).

This did indeed happen in 722 B.C. when the king of Assyria conquered Israel and carried many people into exile.

One may ask why Amos was so certain of this catastrophe. Perhaps the answer can be learned both from the visions which he received and from the nature of the accusations which he made against Israel. In his five visions the threat to the land became darker and darker. In his first vision (Amos 7:1–3) he was shown locusts eating up the grass of the land, and he realized that God was warning him of the destruction of the people and their land. Like a true prophet he interceded for the people.

> O Lord God, forgive, I beseech thee!
> How can Jacob stand?
> He is so small.

The Lord repented concerning this.

"It shall not be," said the Lord (Amos 7:1–3).

The second vision revealed a "judgment by fire, and it

devoured the great deep and was eating up the land" (Amos
7:4–6). Again the prophet interceded with the selfsame
words, and the Lord repented. The third vision showed the
Lord measuring the righteousness of Israel, like an architect
measuring a building, but he found Israel deficient and he
determined to destroy her.

Behold, I am setting a plumb line in the midst of my people
Israel; I will never again pass by them; the high places of Isaac
shall be made desolate, and the sanctuaries of Israel shall be
laid waste, and I will rise against the house of Jeroboam with
the sword (Amos 7:8–9).

That time the prophet did not intercede for the people;
God's threat was final.

In the fourth vision Amos was shown that the end was
near. He was shown a basket of summer fruit and he was
told, "The end has come upon my people Israel" (Amos 8:2).
In the fifth vision (Amos 9:1–10) Amos sees the Lord in the
process itself of destroying the very totality of Israel. The
vehemence of this vision of destruction was of terrifying
aspect, especially if, as is probable, it was delivered at a
sanctuary during a religious festival.

Smite the capitals until the thresholds shake,
    and shatter them on the heads of all the people;
and what are left of them I will slay with the sword;
    not one of them shall flee away,
    not one of them shall escape.
Though they dig into Sheol,
    from there shall my hand take them;
though they climb up to heaven,
    from there I will bring them down.

Though they hide themselves on the top of Carmel,
from there I will search out and take them;
and though they hide from my sight at the bottom of the sea,
there I will command the serpent, and it shall bite them.
And though they go into captivity before their enemies,
there I will command the sword, and it shall slay them;
and I will set my eyes upon them for
evil and not for good (Amos 9:1-4).

One may ask what Israel had done that such dreadful punishment should be inflicted on her. For an answer to this we turn to the main burden of the book of Amos.

The beginning of Amos' message was skillful in its psychology. He began by castigating the foreign nations around Israel as if they were more blameworthy than Israel. He spoke against Damascus, the capital of Syria, because of its crimes of cruelty against the people of Israel (Gilead) and prophesied divine wrath (fire) against the leaders of the Syrians and against the Philistines (Gaza) because they had carried people into slavery and against Phoenicia (Tyre) because they had dishonored a covenant. Up to this point he had spoken against non-Israelite nations, and Amos' hearers may well have thought that they were going to escape judgment. But then Amos proceeded to reprimand Edom and Moab, who were partially Israelitic in origin, because of their brotherly hostility, their cruelty in war, and their desecration of the dead.

It is only in Chapter 2 that we find that Amos had turned to Israel herself. He denounced Judah, and his accusation was that she had neglected the law of the Lord. A climax was reached when he turned to Israel, the Northern Kingdom; her crimes were chiefly injustice toward the poor, unchastity, and sacrilegious behavior. At this point Amos rose as a fierce defendant of the Mosaic law and the covenant of Yahweh. In his accusation we discover direct references to the social laws set down now in the Pentateuch. By their injustice toward the poor they have broken God's precepts.

You shall not pervert the justice due to your poor in his suit. Keep far from a false charge, and do not slay the innocent and righteous, for I will not acquit the wicked. And you shall take no bribe, for a bribe blinds the officials, and subverts the cause of those who are in the right (Ex. 23:6–8; *compare* Deut. 16:18–20).

By keeping garments in pledge (Amos 2:8) they had broken God's commandment.

If ever you take your neighbor's garment in pledge, you shall restore it to him before the sun goes down; for that is his only covering; it is his mantle for his body; in what else shall he sleep? And if he cries to me, I will hear, for I am compassionate (Ex. 22:26).

Because of the direct infringement of these precepts of the Book of the Covenant, Amos knew that destruction would come upon Israel, as it was written in Deuteronomy 28:15–68.

Amos saw the enormity of Israel's crimes in the face of the special benefits which God had given his people when he had brought them out of Egypt and had driven the non-Israelite people out of the land of Canaan for them and given them prophets and Nazirites (Amos 2:9–11). But in spite of all this they had turned aside. Then Amos appealed to the promise of election made to Abraham (Gen. 12:1–3).

You only have I known of all the families of the earth (Amos 3:2).

He then appealed to the covenant.

Do two walk together unless they have made an appointment? (Amos 3:3).

But instead of living in holiness and righteousness in response to their privileged position they were living a life of luxury (Amos 4:4–5 and 5:21–24). God had warned them by repeated disasters, famine, drought, mildew, and plague, but they did not take the warning and return to him (Amos 4:6–11) and now they were faced with destruction. In Chapter 5 Amos did something which must have been terrifying to the Israelites; he sang a dirge or lamentation over Israel, almost like a prophetic ôth, so that the people may well have thought that he was bringing this very thing to pass.

Hear this word which I take up over you in lamentation, O house of Israel: "Fallen, no more to rise, is the virgin Israel; forsaken on her land, with none to raise her up" (Amos 5:1–2).

The mourning theme rose to a crescendo in the theme of the Day of the Lord which the people expected as a day of political and material prosperity and supereminence for Israel. Amos told them that it would not be so; it would be a day when God destroyed rather than exalted the nation.

Woe to you who desire the day of the Lord!
    Why should you have the day of the Lord?
It is darkness, and not light;
    as if a man fled from a lion,
and a bear met him;
    or went into the house and leaned with his hand against the wall,
    and a serpent bit him.

Is not the day of the Lord darkness, and not light,
and gloom with no brightness in it? (Amos 5:18–20).

The prophet Amos has in truth been called the prophet of doom. He brought into vivid relief both the privileged position of Israel, in view of God's care throughout history of the chosen people, but also the dire consequence of Israel's infringement of those privileges, her breaking (or dishonoring) the covenant pledge. Amos stood first in the long line of prophets whose support for the covenant has been committed to writing. Then Jesus himself came to epitomize all the messages of the prophets.

Many scholars have seen no hope in the message of Amos, but at least two passages do show hope. Perhaps they do not belong to Amos, but it is difficult to see why the prophet should have preached at all if he saw no hope of the nation's repentance. In Amos 3:12 we catch a glance of the great theology of the remnant, namely, however bad the nation becomes, a remnant will still remain faithful and be saved by the Lord.

Thus says the Lord: "As the shepherd rescues from the mouth of the lion two legs, or a piece of an ear, so shall the people of Israel who dwell in Samaria be rescued, with the corner of a couch and part of a bed" (Amos 3:12).

Whoever compiled the book of Amos also allowed a message of hope to stand at the very end of the book. In this God promised that, after the destruction of Assyria, the days would come when the house of David would be restored, and the land would become abundantly fertile, and Israel, returned from exile, would dwell safely in her land, which God had given her.

"I will plant them upon their land, and they shall never again be plucked up out of the land which I have given them," says the Lord your God (Amos 9:15).

When we turn to the next prophet, Hosea, we find this everlasting covenant love of Yaweh vividly and dramatically portrayed.

FURTHER READING

Cripps, R. S., *The Book of Amos*. Macmillan, London, 1929.

Morgenstern, J., *Amos Studies*. Hebrew Union College Press, Cincinnati, 1941.

Snaith, N. H., *Amos*. Epworth Press, London, 1945/1946.

Sutcliffe, T. H., *The Book of Amos*. S.P.C.K., London, 1955.

10 Hosea and the Unfaithful Wife

St. Francis de Sales once said that one could "draw more flies by a teaspoonful of honey than a vat of vinegar." Whereas it would be unjust to impute the term "vinegar" to the magnificent poetry of Amos, yet it is not without reason that one can contrast the bitterness,[1] irony,[2] and anger of Amos with the sweetness of Hosea.

HOSEA'S MESSAGE

Hosea was a near contemporary of Amos but he lived in the Northern Kingdom, Israel. He may have been a middle-class tradesman with some education. In Hosea's days it seems that there was slightly less prosperity and a certain amount of political insecurity in the country. Jeroboam II died; his successor, Zechariah, reigned for six months, then Shallum for a month, then Menahem for ten years. During this time of unrest some people were seeking help from Egypt, and others looked for assistance from Assyria.

Hosea faced a religious situation, which was as bad as or perhaps worse than that which confronted Amos. In Israel at that time, the cult of the god Baal was popular. It was a

---

[1] Amos 4:1–3—his bitterness and rudeness toward the indolent women of Samaria, even calling them "cows of Bashan!"

[2] Amos 4:4–5 and 5:4–7—his sarcasm concerning hypercritical worship.

licentious cult centered around Ashtoroth, the goddess of fertility, and her consort El. Ashtoroth in Canaanite literature is depicted as sensual and savage. Figurines, which have been excavated, show an emphasis on her sexual nature; she is sometimes represented as a cow-deity. Canaanite religion followed the cycle of the seasons and involved a type of sympathetic magic whereby there was an attempt to make the gods of fertility awaken or even to resurrect (cf. Hos. 2; 5). As nature died with the summer drought, so it was thought that the god of fertility died. Thus, by sacred prostitution, that is, by inducing life within the womb of a female, the god was supposed to initiate new life in the spring. Such practices were, of course, forbidden in the Hebrew religion.

There shall be no cult prostitute of the daughters of Israel, neither shall there be a cult prostitute of the sons of Israel. You shall not bring the hire of a harlot, or the wages of a dog [sodomite], into the house of the Lord your God in payment of any vow; for both of these are an abomination to the Lord your God (Deut. 23:17–18).

It would seem that the Israelites were indulging in such practices with all their lust and demoralization in the time of Hosea.

My people inquire of a thing of wood, and their staff gives them oracles. For a spirit of harlotry has led them astray, and they have left their God to play the harlot. They sacrifice on the tops of the mountains, and make offerings upon the hills. . . . Therefore your daughters play the harlot, and your brides commit adultery (Hos. 4:12–13).

In the Baal cult man tried to obtain power over the god, but Hosea realized the futility of this, for only Yahweh can bring

life. He is the God over nature and he is the God of history
(Hos. 2:5–13).

Against this background Hosea tried to teach the people
about their apostasy from Yahweh in terms which they
could understand. Or possibly, as we shall see below, by the
experience of his own life he learned to reflect on Israel's
disloyalty to Yahweh and to see her faithlessness in the
poignant terms of adultery. His own life, as far as we can
see, was a prophetic symbol in itself.

From Chapters 1 to 3 we understand either that Hosea
was told to take a temple prostitute or an ordinary prostitute
and reform her; or perhaps his own wife went astray and he
was told to take her back and reform her.

When the Lord first spoke through Hosea, the Lord said to
Hosea, "Go, take to yourself a wife of harlotry . . . for the land
commits great harlotry by forsaking the Lord" (Hos. 1:2).[3]

By Hosea's acceptance of this task he taught the people that
God would also take back Israel and reform her as his bride.

Hosea's children were also prophetic symbols. His first
child was named Jezreel. Jezreel had been the scene of great
battles (Judg. 4:13; 6:33 ff.; 7:1 ff.; 1 Sam. 29:1 ff.; 31), and
in this way God and Hosea indicated to the people that the
fate and future of Israel were about to be decided. As Israel
had punished her enemies, so would God punish Israel.
Hosea's next child was called "Not pitied." The name is full
of meaning, for God had pitied Israel on Mount Sinai and
had answered Moses' request that he should see God's glory.

---

[3] An Israelite did not always take back a woman who had had coition
with another man (cf. Deut. 24:1–4).

And he said, "I will make all my goodness pass before you, and will proclaim before you my name 'The Lord'; and I will be gracious to whom I will be gracious, and will show mercy on whom I will show mercy" (Ex. 33:19).

Hosea's second child, like the first, showed the complete reversal of Israel's fortune; as she was victor, so she will be vanquished, as she was pitied, so she will be unpitied. The name of the third child, "Not my people" (*v.* 8), portrayed also a reversal of the inheritance at the Exodus—there God had promised that Israel would be his people; Hosea's third child represents the repudiation of this promise.

Through this imagery Hosea wished to teach at least two important truths. First he taught that Israel was God's son.

When Israel was a child, I loved him, and out of Egypt I called my son (Hos. 11:1).

Compare this with

And you shall say to Pharaoh, "Thus says the Lord, Israel is my first-born son, and I say to you, 'Let my son go that he may serve me'" (Ex. 4:22).

Second, Hosea taught that Israel was God's bride.

Then she shall say, "I will go and return to my first husband" (Hos. 2:7).

And in that day, says the Lord, you will call me, "My husband," and no longer will you call me, "My Baal" (Hos. 2:16).

I will betroth you to me in faithfulness; and you shall know the
Lord (Hos. 2:20).

The two ideas or expressions of relationship are comple-
mentary. The idea of "son" denotes the election of Israel on
the part of God; and the idea of "bride," the free choice of
the covenant by Israel. In these two notions are exquisitely
balanced the twin concepts of human freedom and divine
predestination. The concept of *hesed* is prominent in Hosea;
on the side of God it denotes pure, gratuitous love and
cherishing grace in a strong bond of loyalty; on Israel's side
it demands love and obedience.

The breaking or dishonoring of the covenant was nothing
less than adultery, and Israel through this adultery became
a harlot. She went so far astray from God that God could
say, ". . . for she is not my wife, and I am not her husband"
(Hos. 2:2). But God, like Hosea, was ready to go and love
his wife again.

And the Lord said to me, "Go again, love a woman who is
beloved of a paramour and is an adulteress; even as the Lord
loves the people of Israel, though they turn to other gods and
love cakes of raisins" (Hos. 3:1).

Hosea looked forward to a time when Israel would be
"reeducated" as in the days of discipline in the desert
(Hos. 2:14–15; 3:3–5), after which a return like a new
exodus and entry into the Promised Land through the
valley of Achor (*compare* Josh. 7) would occur. Hosea
anticipates the perfect union of God and Israel and foretells
the redemption of all nature. "In that day God will make
a covenant not only with Israel, but also with the whole of
his creation, animate and inanimate alike, with both the

beasts of the field and with the corn and the wine and the oil."[4] This suggests a reversal of Genesis 3:17–19 and a return to the peace and prosperity of paradise.

In Hosea we see God depicted almost wholly as a God of intense love entering into the sphere of history and suffering pain and anguish over his beloved. Sin is primarily an ugly betrayal of love rather than the simple breaking of a moral law. In a transcendent human relationship we are able to catch a glimpse of God's love. Hosea's book anticipates the redemptive love of Christ for the Church as his bride. For Hosea the Day of Yahweh is a day of light when the remnant is saved.

FURTHER READING

Snaith, N. H., *Amos, Hosea and Micah.* Allenson, Naperville, Ill., 1956.

---

[4] G. A. F. Knight, *Hosea* (*Torch Bible Commentaries*, ed. by J. March, D. M. Paton, and A. Richardson) (Allenson, Naperville, Ill., 1966), p. 26.

11 The Faithful Wife: The Song of Solomon

Rabbi Akiba (first century A.D.) wrote of the Song of Solomon,

... for all the ages are not worth the day on which the Song of Songs was given to Israel; for all the Writings are holy, but the Song of Songs is the Holy of Holies ... (*Mishnah, Yadaim,* 3:5).[1]

The Song of Solomon is perhaps the most difficult book in the whole of the bible. It was probably a collection of erotic poems or poems celebrating a wedding. Some have suggested that Chapters 6:4–7:9 were sung as the bride performed the Mahanaim dance, probably the war or sword dance. But if this book merely contains love songs, why was it included in the bible? It is true that one could say that it is sufficient that it celebrated and confirmed the Hebrew idea that marriage and physical coition are especially holy, not only ordained but also commanded by God when he said,

Be fruitful and multiply, and fill the earth and subdue it (Gen. 1:28).

[1] H. Danby, *The Mishnah* (Clarendon Press, Oxford, 1933), used with permission.

Speaking of the importance of marriage, the Jewish teachers said,

He who is without a wife dwells without blessing, life, joy, help, good and peace. . . . See how important a thing marriage is, for God has united His name with marriage, in the Law, in the Prophets, and in the Holy Writing. . . .[2]

Yet even the Jews with their exalted view of marriage were not content to interpret the Song of Solomon literally. Very early they began to see a deeper meaning in the Song, and we find the Aramaic paraphrase (the Targum) of it interpreting the whole Song in terms of Israel's history: under the figures of human love the Song set forth the story of God's dealings with his chosen people. Some scholars show that the first half is the story of Israel from the exodus to the time of Solomon; the second half, Israel's defection from God, the exile, after that the restoration to God's favor, and then the rebuilding of the Temple, which had been destroyed in the sixth century B.C.

YAHWEH AND HIS BRIDE

If this is so, and it seems the most probable conclusion, then the Song of Solomon is woven around the story of the covenant love between Yahweh and his bride, Israel. This is the interpretation of the early Jewish commentators. Let us take a few examples.

The rabbis pictured God electing Israel while she was working in bricks and mortar in Egypt.

Come with me from Lebanon, my bride, with me (Song 4:8).

[2] Midrash on the Psalms, lix, (151a para. 2).

The Jewish teachers commented,

A virgin is allowed twelve months from the time the bridegroom claims her to prepare herself for the wedding. I [God], however, did not observe this rule, but while you were still busy with the bricks and mortar I hastened to redeem you [here the commentator sees a play on the Hebrew word for "bricks" and the word "Lebanon," which are similar] (*Cant. R.* 4:8).

So this was the beginning of the courtship of Israel. The Jewish teachers pictured Israel as "sick with love" (Song. 5:8) in Egypt and then meetng God at the Red Sea when his heart was "ravished" (Song 4:9) by the sight of Israel. Then they saw the actual wedding taking place on Mount Sinai. Rabbi Johanan interpreted the verse, "O that you would kiss me with the kiss of your mouth" (Song 1:2), as applying to Israel when she went up Mount Sinai.

It was as if a king wanted to marry a wife of good and noble family, so he sent an envoy to speak with her. She said: "I am not worthy to be his handmaid, but all the same I desire to hear from his own mouth." When the envoy returned to the king, he was full of smiles, but he would give no clear report to the king. The king, who was very discerning, said: "This man is full of smiles, which would show that she consented, and he does not give any clear report, which would seem to show that she said that she wants to hear from my own mouth." So Israel is the woman of good family, Moses is the envoy, and the king is the Holy One, blessed be He (*Song of Songs Rabbah*, 1, 2, 3).

Thus, Israel was depicted sleeping on Mount Sinai—very lightly like a gazelle—while Moses, the bridegroom's friend, and God, the bridegroom, came down the mountain to effect the union with Israel. Israel consented to the union when she said,

All that the Lord has spoken we will do (Ex. 19:8).

About midnight God came and perfected the nuptials so the Day of Sinai was known as the Day of Espousals.

In the day of his espousals [Song 3:11]: this was the day of Sinai, when Israel were like bridegrooms. *And in the day of the gladness of his heart* [Song 3:11]: this refers to [when they received] the Torah, as it says, *The precepts of the Lord are right, rejoicing the heart* (*Song of Songs Rabbah,* III, 11:2).

Sometimes the consecration of the tent of meeting[3] was called the Day of Espousals because the cloud, signifying God's presence, descended on the tent (Ex. 33:10), and Israel thought of the tent as the bridal chamber.

Sometimes the Day of Sinai was thought of as the marriage between God as bridegroom and Israel as bride, or sometimes between Israel as bridegroom and the Torah (the law) as bride. Either idea expresses the covenant relationship between God and Israel under the same symbols and expressions that the prophet Hosea employed. But the Song of Solomon is not the story of an adulterous Israel but of a faithful Israel, who loves God with all the passion of a young bride, and God, who reciprocates that love.

It is this theme which the synoptic evangelists took up when they spoke of Jesus as the bridegroom.

And Jesus said to them, "Can the wedding guests mourn as long as the bridegroom is with them? The days will come, when the bridegroom is taken away from them, and then they will fast" (Mt. 9:15; *compare* Mk. 2:19 ff.; Lk. 5:34 ff.).

He who has the bride is the bridegroom; the friend of the bridegroom, who stands and hears him, rejoices greatly at the bride-

---

[3] See Chapter 7, "The Kingly Court."

groom's voice; therefore this joy of mine is now full. He must increase, but I must decrease (Jn. 3:29–30).

This theme closes the bible, the theme of the most exalted and concrete expression of the covenant love between God and the New Israel.

Then I saw a new heaven and a new earth; for the first heaven and the first earth had passed away. . . . And I saw the holy city, new Jerusalem, coming down out of heaven from God, prepared as a bride adorned for her husband; and I heard a great voice from the throne saying, "Behold, the dwelling of God is with men. He will dwell with them, and they shall be his people, and God himself will be with them; he will wipe away every tear from their eyes, and death shall be no more, neither shall there be mourning nor crying nor pain any more, for the former things have passed away" (Rev. 21:1–4).

It is within the transcendent love between men and women that we first catch a glimpse of and experience the idea of perfect union between God and his people in the bond of *hesed*.[4]

FURTHER READING

Buzy, D., "L'allegorie matrimoniale de Jahve et d'Israel et le Cantique des Cantiques." *Vivre et Penser* 3 (1944), pp. 77-90.

Dubarle, A. M., "L'Amour Humain dans le Cantique des Cantiques." *Revue Biblique* 61 (1953), pp. 67-86.

Murphy, R. E., "Recent Literature on the Canticle of Canticles." *Catholic Biblical Quarterly* 16 (1954), pp. 1-11.

Rowley, H. H., "The Interpretation of the Song of Songs." *The Servant of the Lord*. Lutterworth Press, London, 1952, pp. 187-234.

[4] As Brother Richard Formica expressed it to the author, "Revelation is a deepening communal awareness of the relationship between God and the community."

II   THE NEW TESTAMENT

12 The Last Savior

THE GENEALOGY

St. Matthew begins his Gospel with the verse,

The book of the genealogy of Jesus Christ, the son of David, the son of Abraham (Mt. 1:1).

This verse carries our minds back immediately to the covenant with Abraham, the father of the Jewish people. St. Matthew means us to realize that Jesus' coming is the fulfillment of the covenant with Abraham. Jesus is the awaited "seed" of Abraham, which God promised in Genesis 17:1–8.

When Abram was ninety-nine years old the Lord appeared to Abram, and said to him, "I am God Almighty; walk before me, and be blameless. And I will make my covenant between me and you, and will multiply you exceedingly." Then Abram fell on his face; and God said to him, "Behold, my covenant is with you, and you shall be the father of a multitude of nations. No longer shall your name be Abram, but your name shall be Abraham; for I have made you father of a multitude of nations. I will make you exceedingly fruitful; and I will make nations of you, and kings shall come forth from you. And I will establish my covenant between me and you and your descendants after you throughout their generations for an everlasting covenant, to be God to you and to your descendants after you. And I will give to you, and to your descendants after you, the land of your sojourning, all the land of Canaan, for an everlasting possession; and I will be their God."

St. Paul comments that the correct reading of the other election text (Gen. 12:7) refers to one descendant and that descendant was Jesus.

Now the promises were made to Abraham and to his offspring. It does not say, "And to offsprings," referring to many; but, referring to one, "And to your offspring," which is Christ (Gal. 3:16).

Further the coming of Christ means the fulfillment of the beginning of Genesis 12.

And I will make of you a great nation, and I will bless you, and make your name great, so that you will be a blessing. I will bless those who bless you, and him who curses you I will curse; and by you all the families of the earth shall bless themselves (Gen. 12:2–3).

St. Paul refers to this also and understands it to refer to the incorporation of the Gentiles into the Church.

And the scripture, foreseeing that God would justify the Gentiles by faith, preached the gospel beforehand to Abraham, saying, "In you shall all the nations be blessed." So then, those who are men of faith are blessed with Abraham who had faith (Gal. 3:8–9).

St. Matthew, therefore, in the genealogy of Jesus, which he gives in Chapter 1:1–16, shows that the foundation of the Church is clearly rooted in the family of Abraham because of the promises made to him by God.

St. Matthew's genealogy falls into three parts, each of fourteen generations. The first part (*vv.* 2–6a) traces the Jewish people up to the time of King David. The second part (*vv.* 6b–11) enumerates the descendants of King David and portrays the maintenance of the Davidic kingship until its fall at the time of the conquest of Israel by the Babylonians in the sixth century B.C., when many of the Jews were carried into exile. The third part (*vv.* 12–16) lists David's descendants from the deportation to Babylon to the time when Jesus was born.

St. Matthew summarizes all this in verse 17:

So all the generations from Abraham to David were fourteen generations, and from David to the deportation to Babylon fourteen generations, and from the deportation to Babylon to the Christ fourteen generations.

Clearly, we must see this genealogy as being rather artificial in that St. Matthew obviously has omitted some of Jesus' descendants; in a typically Hebrew manner everything must be in neat, round numbers. Nevertheless, his theological point is clear—Jesus is a true son of Abraham and he is from the house of David. But Jesus is from the house of David through Joseph his foster father, not through Mary, his physical mother.[1] To us at the present time this may appear to be rather strange, but it is not to the non-Western mind. Legally Jesus was of the house of David through Joseph, even though Joseph had no part in his physical generation.

Perhaps an example from Africa might help to illustrate this. In some tribes in Rhodesia (the Malaki), for example,

---

[1] *Compare* the promise to Abraham and Sarah, namely, ". . . kings shall come forth from thee" (Gen. 17:6). A "b" by the side of the number of the verse means the second part of the verse.

there exists the following custom. If a boy or a man dies *without* marrying, then his brother takes a wife for the dead man and physically generates and raises up children who belong to the "ghost," and the inheritance of the ghost goes to them and not to the brother. Although the ghost has had no part at all in the physical generation of the children and, indeed, had not even a wife before he died, legally he has children. The brother, who has generated the children, must take a second woman in order to raise up children of his own, or if he dies before he is able to do so, another brother takes a wife for him and so the ghost marriages continue. This is a very good example of legal sonship without any physical contact or rites of adoption.

The importance which St. Matthew attaches to the Jewish heritage of Jesus may be seen if we look at the genealogy of Jesus which is given by St. Luke. In Luke 3:23–38 we find a list of Jesus' ancestors traced from Joseph right back to Adam, "the son of God." Now no one could possibly have kept accurate records of ancestors from Adam! But, just as in Matthew, St. Luke's theological point is clear. He wished to present Jesus as the Savior of the whole human race, the second Adam (*compare* 1 Cor. 15:45). Also, complementing St. Matthew, Luke wanted to show the priesthood of Christ by noting his connection with Levi (*v.* 24).

THE WOMEN IN THE GENEALOGY

We must mention one more thing before we leave the genealogy of St. Matthew. He does something which is quite strange for one who is recording a genealogy. He includes four women in the list.

In Matthew 1:3 we find a reference to Tamar, whose story is recorded in Genesis 38. In the Old Testament days, and even today in many cultures, it was regarded as highly important, indeed, almost imperative, that men should beget children. Indeed, the first commandment given in the bible is "Be fruitful and multiply and fill the earth" (Gen. 1:28). Tamar's husband died, and her relatives were supposed to raise up children to the dead man by cohabiting with Tamar. This they refused to do. So Tamar disguised herself as a prostitute, and her father-in-law succumbed to temptation and went in to her. Tamar secured his signet, his cord, and his staff from him as a proof that it was he who had made her pregnant. She was therefore saved from the capital punishment meted out for adultery, and an ancestor of Christ was born.

In 1:5 are mentioned Rahab and Ruth. Rahab was the woman who hid the Israelite spies when they came to reconnoiter Jericho before Joshua and the people captured it. On account of her kindness the spies promised to save her and her house if she distinguished it by tying a red cord outside. Her house was saved (Josh. 6), and according to one extrabiblical tradition she married Joshua! Whether this is true or not, it shows that Matthew was not adverse to including non-Israelite people in the community of the chosen people.

Ruth was a Moabite who had lost her husband and was childless. A kinsman, Boaz, took her as his wife to raise up children in her husband's name according to the Jewish levirate law, whereby a relative was expected to take the widow of a kinsman and keep his name alive by raising up children for him. Ruth, perhaps, may be described as a woman of half-Israelite blood, for the Moabites were supposedly descendants of Ishmael, the son of Abraham by his wife's bondswoman, Hagar.

The next woman to be mentioned is "the wife of Uriah"

(Mt. 1:6b). This woman's name was Bathsheba. David fell in love with her, contrived and succeeded in having Uriah killed in the front line of battle, and then married Bathsheba (2 Sam. 11:1–12:25). There is no disguising the fact that David (and Bathsheba) committed sin; the Jews call this "the unnameable sin." Nathan the prophet revealed David's sin to him by telling him the following parable:

"There were two men in a certain city, the one rich and the other poor. The rich man had very many flocks and herds; but the poor man had nothing but one little ewe lamb, which he had bought. And he brought it up, and it grew up with him and with his children; it used to eat of his morsel, and drink from his cup, and lie in his bosom, and it was like a daughter to him. Now there came a traveler to the rich man, and he was unwilling to take one of his own flock or herd to prepare for the wayfarer who had come to him, but he took the poor man's lamb, and prepared it for the man who had come to him." Then David's anger was greatly kindled against the man; and he said to Nathan, "As the Lord lives, the man who has done this deserves to die; and he shall restore the lamb fourfold, because he did this thing, and because he had no pity." Nathan said to David, "You are the man" (2 Sam. 12:1–7).

David repented of his sin but he lost the child conceived by Bathsheba before they married. God forgave David and gave him another son, Solomon, after his repentance. Perhaps St. Matthew meant to remind us of the mercy of God toward the repentant sinner, a point illustrated in the parable of the Good Shepherd searching for the one lost lamb. God would not let one man's sin prevent his covenant love.

It seems as if St. Matthew introduced these women for several reasons. First, to show how the providence of God overruled adverse circumstances in order to fulfill his purpose in salvation history; second, to show that women, as well as men, have a distinctive role to play in redemption; third, to show the Gentiles and half-Jews entering into the covenant of the chosen people; and fourth, but not least, to move toward the great figure of Mary.[2]

THE VIRGINAL CONCEPTION OF JESUS

Matthew 1:18–25 tells us of the virginal conception of Jesus by Mary, his mother. St. Luke supplements these details in his narrative of the annunciation (Lk. 1:26–38); St. Mark and St. John do not speak about the infancy of Jesus. Some scholars have compared the infancy narratives of Matthew and Luke to pagan myths about virginal conceptions and virgin births. These scholars compare the infancy narratives with Greek mythology. However, their arguments do not appear to be wholly convincing as Professor C. K. Barrett and others have shown. Very often the mothers of these wonder children were far from models of ladylike modesty; the figures themselves, for example, the goddesses, were usually from the realm of myth and fantasy. There is little correspondence between the details of Jesus' birth and these stories.

It is becoming increasingly obvious to scholars that the beginnings of the Gospels of Matthew and Luke, as well as the beginning of the Acts, were written from a Semitic background and possibly in the Aramaic language (the language probably spoken by Jesus) and not from Greek sources. If the writers of these Gospels wished to draw on stories rather than historical facts, they had plenty of "hero and heroine"

[2] One might also comment that Matthew's genealogy illustrates how harlots and sinners enter into the kingdom of heaven.

stories about the Jewish patriarchs and matriarchs for their sources. Indeed, as we shall see, they added certain details from these.

It would seem, therefore, that we cannot doubt that there was a historical basis for the basic facts of Jesus' conception and birth. However, these fundamental facts did not preclude the evangelist from weaving into his narrative details which, though not necessarily historical, through "poetic licence" illustrate a theological truth.

The virginal conception of Jesus by Mary is the culmination of God's particular providence for the women whom he elected to play a part in salvation history. He intervened on behalf of Sarah, Rachel, Rebecca, and Hannah, the mother of the prophet Samuel, in order to give them the children of destiny when they were naturally sterile.[3]

We shall note that throughout his Gospel Matthew is very interested in bringing before our eyes a Jesus who is the fulfillment of the type of Moses. Any affinity which Matthew can find between the history and traditions surrounding Moses and the history and traditions about Jesus he introduces into his Gospel. Deuteronomy 18:15 foretold that a prophet like Moses would appear. There is a tradition about Moses which cannot be traced historically, but which may cast light on the reason why St. Matthew chose to include the detail of the virginal conception of Jesus.

According to this tradition, at the time when Pharaoh wished to destroy the children of Israel in Egypt, the Jewish men abstained from their wives. In the Jewish law there is a counsel advising men with children to abstain from marital coition during catastrophes, such as a famine. This absten-

---

[3] Sterility may have been exceedingly common in the ancient world owing to disease and incorrect diet. In countries of low economic standard today it is not uncommon for as many as 40% of the women to be sterile.

tion they called "affliction of soul." In Exodus 2:24–25 it is
said,

And God heard their groaning, and God remembered his covenant with Abraham, with Isaac, and with Jacob. And God saw the
people of Israel, and God knew . . .

The Jewish teachers interpreted the word "knew" in a
nuptial sense; they said that God saw the abstinence of
Moses' father and he intervened to make Moses' mother
conceive. This does not mean that there was a virginal
conception but only that God intervened miraculously to
give Jochebed a special child.

God, as it were, goes one step further in the conception of
Jesus. Jesus is conceived by a virgin who does not *know* man
at all. The child conceived is to be a second Moses, the Last
Deliverer of his people, the prophet foretold in Deuteronomy
18:15.

The Lord your God will raise up for you a prophet like me from
among you, from your brethren—him shall you heed. . . .

In Matthew 1:18–25 Mary is described as betrothed to
Joseph, but they have not engaged in marital coition. According to Jewish law Mary was legally the spouse of
Joseph although only the betrothal had been implemented.
She would have needed a bill of divorce to be separated from
Joseph; and, although coition was not normally practiced
during betrothal, a child conceived during that time was
considered legitimate. Joseph, discovering that she was with
child, resolved to put her away quietly. He was obliged to
separate from her, for a strict Jew would not marry a woman
who had been impregnated by another man. On betrothal

a woman was regarded as set aside for one man "as a vessel
in the sanctuary for God." Joseph learned in a supernatural
way that Mary had not been defiled and that her son would
be called Jesus (the same name as Joshua), for "he will save
his people from their sins."[4]

St. Matthew, then, sees this event as the fulfillment of the
prophecy of Isaiah 7:14.

Behold, a virgin shall conceive and bear a son, and his name
shall be called Emmanuel (Mt. 1:23).

This does not mean that the prophet Isaiah was actually
prophesying the virginal conception of Jesus. Indeed, the
Hebrew word *almah* is a general word meaning "young
woman." Matthew looked back and realized that Isaiah's
prophecy had a deeper meaning than the prophet himself
understood. Matthew understood the word to mean "virgin."
By the time Jesus rose from the dead the full import of "God
with us" (which is the meaning of Emmanuel) must have
been realized.

In Matthew 1:25 we learn that Joseph did not know Mary
"until she had borne a son; and he called his name Jesus."
There has been much controversy about the word "until."
Recent discoveries of Greek papyri suggest—although we
cannot be certain—that it might be possible to translate this
verse as follows: "He did not know her even when she
brought forth a son . . ." It is possible that Joseph thought
that he was bound by the Jewish law (*compare* Deut.

---

[4] It is perhaps possible that Mary underwent a "medical examination"
conducted by women (*compare* the "pregnant virgin" in the Babylonian
Talmud, *Hagigah* 14–15). The rabbis were not scrupulous about discussing
intimate details of sexual life. A woman used "test rags" to discover whether
she was ritually clean before coition, and it is reported also that the strict
Pharisees required women to show the color of their menstrual discharge.

24:1–4) which stated that a man must not have coitus with his wife if she has been impregnated or has been in a position where this was a danger, for example, as a war captive. Even if the woman had not been raped, the man did not have coitus with her but just financially supported her. This was especially observed by those of the priestly caste. On the other hand, Joseph may well have abstained from Mary from a sense of religious awe in that her uterus had been the abode of the Elect One. There is no clear indication that Joseph knew Jesus was God.

Thus, St. Matthew at the beginning of his Gospel picked up several themes of the Old Testament, which we have already encountered. These are the promises to Abraham and Sarah; the inclusion of the Gentiles and sinners in the chosen people; and the theme of the Prophet, like Moses, who was expected to come. Chapter 1 of Matthew is alive with the expectation that that which had been foreshadowed in the Old Testament was about to be brought forth. God's everlasting covenant with his elected people was to be fulfilled in Christ.

13 Jesus, the Personification of Israel

In order to study the following sections with facility it is advisable to use a synopsis or harmony of the Gospels. Synopsis does not mean "summary" in our modern sense of "synopsis of the radio news" but something "seen" (*-opsis*) "together" (*syn-*, with). The first three Gospels, Matthew, Mark, and Luke, are similar in so many ways that one can place them in parallel columns and examine their similarities and dissimilarities. By noting the differences we see the individual theology of each evangelist. At one time scholars stressed the entire difference of John from the synoptic evangelists (as Matthew, Mark, and Luke are called), but modern scholars are beginning to emphasize features common to John and the synoptics, especially those between Luke and John.

In this chapter we will study John the Baptist and the baptism of Jesus, taking St. Matthew's Gospel and comparing and contrasting it with the others. Then, we shall consider Christ's temptations.

JOHN THE BAPTIST AND HIS MESSAGE

John the Baptist stands, as it were, at the end of the Old Testament and on the threshold of the New. He appeared in the wilderness of Judea, preaching a message of repentance

120

to the people. His appearance is not unlike that of the prophet, Elijah. He apparently was living the simple life of the desert nomad. Some scholars have suggested that John the Baptist belonged to the group of Jewish people who lived near the Dead Sea in the area called Qumran. These people seem to have been Jews who rejected the Jerusalem priesthood. The priesthood had, indeed, become rather corrupt owing to the influence of Greek culture and customs, an influence developing from about the second century B.C. This group of Jews had retired into the desert region[1] to live a life in close conformity to the law of Moses, to relive as closely as possible the life, experience, and expectation of the Israelites in the desert. There was a section of the community which was fairly exclusive and kept apart from the common people. But John may have belonged to the division of the community which lived in the towns and villages around the region of the Dead Sea and which was permitted to travel and discourse with people who did not belong to the Qumran community. Thus, John would have been able to perform his mission.

John appeared preaching repentance, a theme popular among the Qumran Covenanters—he used a text of interest to them. St. Matthew reports that John cited Isaiah 40:3:

> The voice of one crying in the wilderness:
> Prepare the way of the Lord,
> make his paths straight (Mt. 3:3).

St. Mark combines this text with one from Malachi 3:1:

---

[1] For more information about these people see G. Vermes, *The Dead Sea Scrolls in English* (Penguin Books, Baltimore, 1962). This gives an introduction concerning the Qumran community and a translation of the writings they used.

Behold, I send my messenger before thy face (Mk. 1:2).

St. Luke cites Isaiah 40, but he takes the text further than
St. Matthew by adding,

> Every valley shall be filled,
>   and every mountain and hill shall be brought low,
>   and the crooked shall be made straight,
>   and the rough ways shall be made smooth;
>   and all flesh shall see the salvation of God (Lk. 3:5–6).

From these variations we can see that the evangelists
meant to indicate the main theme of John's preaching,
without confining him to one or two verses from Isaiah. In
the time of Christ many Jews were well versed in the bible
and many knew the sacred words by heart. Thus, it was
quite sufficient for a writer or preacher or teacher to quote
one verse, and the hearers would realize that he was referring to a whole section of scripture. We know, therefore, that
John the Baptist was preaching on the text of Isaiah, but we
do not know the exact length of the section on which he
preached.

If we turn to this whole section in Isaiah, we find that it
is the beginning of what we call Second or Deutero-Isaiah[2]
and it concerns the coming deliverance of Jerusalem. It
begins with

[2] We do not know the name of the person (or persons) who compiled
Isaiah 40–55. The prophecies contained in this portion of the book appear
to emanate from about the sixth century B.C. The coming salvation consists
in God's forgiveness of Israel's sin, the gathering of the exiled people, and
the return to Zion. God's deliverance is described in the terms of a new
creation. The miracles which were wrought first in Egypt will be repeated
in a more wonderful way (Is. 43:lb ff.; 48:21; 51:9 ff.). The Qumran community appears to have been greatly interested in Isaiah.

> Comfort, comfort my people, says your God.
> Speak tenderly to Jerusalem,
>   and cry to her
> that her warfare is ended,
>   that her iniquity is pardoned,
> that she has received from the Lord's hand
>   double for all her sins (Is. 40:1–2).

Now the main theme of this part of Isaiah is the coming deliverance which will be wrought by God himself and by no other. This future redemption or salvation will take the form of a second exodus, that is, it will be based on the form of the first. But it cannot be overemphasized that the redeemer will be God and he will save Israel from their sins (*compare* Mt. 1:21, where the name of Jesus is explained, "for he will save the people from their sins"). Again and again this occurs in Deutero-Isaiah:

... prepare the way of the Lord ... (Is. 40:3).

... say to the cities of Judah, "Behold, your God!" (Is. 40:9b).

I, I am the Lord, and besides me there is no savior (Is. 43:11).

Thus says the Lord, your Redeemer, the Holy One of Israel ... send it forth to the end of the earth; say, "The Lord has redeemed his servant Jacob!" (Is. 48:17, 20).

It is clear, therefore, that the redeemer expected was God himself, in contrast to the Messiah, who generally was considered a human and political figure.[3] Thus, when John the

---

[3] Among the Jewish people there seems to have been a constant belief in a messianic age but not such a constant belief in an individual Messiah. The Qumran community seems to have expected a political Messiah and a priestly Messiah. One must carefully distinguish the Messiah from the Redeemer; for the Jew (and Christian) only God can redeem.

Baptist preached on Isaiah 40, he was probably preparing
the people for him who was to come, most likely realizing
that this would be the Holy One of Israel, though he would
not necessarily identify him with Jesus. He would expect
God to act in a way similar to that in which he did at the
first exodus.

The Qumran Covenanters had used this text of Isaiah and
had interpreted it as follows:

. . . they [the elect] may indeed "go into the wilderness to prepare
the way," i.e., do what Scripture enjoins when it says, "Prepare
in the wilderness the way . . . make straight in the desert a
highway for our God" [Is. 40:3]. [The reference is to the study
of the Law which God commanded through Moses to the end
that, as occasion arises, all things may be done in accordance with
what is revealed therein and with what the prophets also have
revealed through God's holy spirit.][4]

The crux of the preaching of John and of the teaching of
the people of Qumran was a return to the covenant and its
obligations. John appeared, therefore, to be preaching a
baptism of repentance in preparation for the coming of the
Holy One, God. Here it may be apposite to observe that it
has been suggested that St. John may have been preaching
around the Feast of the Day of Atonement, a yearly commemoration of the Day of the Lord, a day of repentance
and renewal which was preceded by purificatory baths,
confession of sin, repentance, satisfaction, and other ritual
acts.

Was John, we wonder, a "popular" preacher whom the
people came out to hear at this special time of the year
when preachers were accustomed to preach sermons of

[4] From *The Dead Sea Scriptures*, translated by Theodor H. Gaster. Copyright © 1956, 1964 by Theodor H. Gaster. Reprinted by permission of
Doubleday & Company, Inc.

teshuvah (repentance). Matthew tells us that "Jerusalem and all Judea and all the region about Jordan" came to him to be baptized and that Pharisees and Sadducees also came. John warned them that they must practice "deeds of loving kindness" and have a genuine religion. If these people came for a baptism, then John's baptism cannot have been the baptism performed for converts to Judaism but something within Judaism itself. St. Luke tells us that John gave special instructions to the tax collectors and soldiers. This was consonant with the practice of the teachers, contemporary with Jesus, who counseled their disciples, as fathers counseled their sons, especially between New Year's Day and the Day of Atonement, a period of ten days.

Such was the reputation of John that people began to wonder whether he was the Messiah, but John repudiated this by replying that one mightier than he was coming, and by adding "the thong of whose sandals I am not worthy to untie" (Lk. 3:16). Recently there has been a suggestion[5] that the Greek text really means that John will take off his sandals in the presence of the one who is mightier than he. This is a very interesting suggestion and would link itself nicely with the exodus motif which recurs so frequently in Matthew. It recalls to our minds Moses before the burning bush, the theophany of Yahweh to the First Deliverer, who was told to remove his sandals before God. John further announced that he who was to come would baptize with the Holy Spirit and with fire. In Deutero-Isaiah, God himself is the dispenser of the Holy Spirit:

I will pour my Spirit upon your descendants, and my blessing on your offspring (Is. 44:3b).

---

[5] Paul G. Bretscher, " 'Whose Sandals?' (Matt. 3:11)," *Journal of Biblical Literature* 86 (1967), pp. 81–87.

Further, his winnowing fork is in his hand, and he will clear his threshing floor and gather his wheat into the granary, "but the chaff he will burn with unquenchable fire" (Lk. 3:17). In the Old Testament this "recompense" is wrought only by God. To the Jew it would be impious to suppose that it could be wrought by man.

To sum up, John the Baptist preached the preparation of a highway for Israel's God. He used the text of Second Isaiah which portrayed the imminent redemption as a second exodus wrought by Yahweh himself. Yahweh had strode through the waters of the Sea of Reeds, and Jesus begins his public activity by passing through the waters of the Jordan. Little by little, Jesus would reveal that he could perform the functions of Yahweh, especially as depicted in Second Isaiah.

JESUS' BAPTISM

When Jesus appeared for baptism, Matthew (but not Mark and Luke) writes that John tried to prevent Jesus, saying,

I need to be baptized by you, and do you come to me?

John recognized Jesus as the one mightier than himself.

Jesus' reply is instructive; he says,

Let it be so now; for thus it is fitting for us to fulfill all righteousness (Mt. 3:15).

Scholars have been exercised about this reply, but a tenable explanation seems to be that Jesus meant that all details of salvation history had to be fulfilled.[6] These details

[6] Cf. W. D. Davies, *The Sermon on the Mount* (Cambridge University Press, London, 1963) pp. 25–93.

were essentially linked to redemption history as seen as the second exodus. Compare this with the quotation from the Qumran documents: ". . . that things may be done in accordance with what is revealed therein and with what the prophets also have revealed through God's holy spirit" (*compare* the Holy Spirit in Jesus' baptism, as above). At his baptism Jesus began to relive in himself the experiences of the children of Israel. He is the corporate personality of Israel, that is, he embodied in himself the whole of Israel. His life was to fulfill what had been foreshadowed by Israel in the Old Testament.

Jesus stepped into the Jordan as the Israelites had crossed both the Red Sea and the Jordan on their way to the Promised Land. The crossing of the Sea had been regarded frequently by the Jews as a kind of baptism. St. Paul adopted this point of view.

I want you to know, brethren, that our fathers were all under the cloud, and all passed through the sea, and all were baptized into Moses in the cloud and in the sea, and all ate the same supernatural food and all drank the same supernatural drink. For they drank from the supernatural Rock which followed them, and the Rock was Christ. Nevertheless with most of them God was not pleased; for they were overthrown in the wilderness (1 Cor. 10:1–5).

As Jesus came up from the water,

the heavens were opened and he saw the Spirit of God descending like a dove and alighting on him; and lo, a voice from heaven, saying, "This is my beloved Son, with whom I am well pleased" (Mt. 3:16–17).

In an ancient Jewish commentary on Exodus the writer

portrayed the children of Israel passing through the Red Sea. He reported a tradition that at that time the Holy Spirit descended upon them, and they received a vision of the heavenly host and were assured of salvation. Jesus, as the New Israel, is pictured as having a similar experience.

The voice from heaven and the descent of the Holy Spirit reflect Isaiah 42:1 and 44:1–3:

> Behold, my servant, whom I uphold,
>   my chosen, in whom my soul delights;
> I have put my Spirit upon him,
>   he will bring forth justice to the nations (Is. 42:1).

> But now hear, O Jacob, my servant,
>   Israel whom I have chosen!
> Thus says the Lord who made you,
>   who formed you from the womb and will help you:
> Fear not, O Jacob my servant,
>   Jeshurun whom I have chosen. . . .
> I will pour my Spirit upon your descendants,
>   and my blessing on your offspring (Is. 44:1–3).

Some manuscripts read that the voice from heaven proclaimed: "You are my son, today I have begotten you." This quotation comes from Psalm 2:7, and thus the voice designated Jesus as the messianic king.

Therefore, Jesus was proclaimed as the Servant of Yahweh, the one about whom Second Isaiah prophesied. We do not know whose sufferings the prophet was describing; it might be his own sufferings, or those of the community, or those of someone in the future, or perhaps all of these together. In Second Isaiah appear four "Servant Songs"; scholars have not decided precisely on their length, but the following are commonly accepted by most scholars: Isaiah 42:1–9; 49:1–6;

50:4–9; 52:13–53:12. Julian Morgenstern has suggested that here the Book of Isaiah is cast in the literary form of drama, and he reconstructs it as follows:[7]

GOD IS THE SPEAKER

42:1 Behold, My servant, on whom I lay hold,
　　　　Mine elect, in whom My soul delights;
　　　I have set My spirit upon him;
　　　　Right order for the nations will he bring forth.

2　　He will not cry out nor will he raise his voice,
　　　　Nor will he let it be heard in the street.

3　　A crushed reed, he will not be broken;
　　　　Yea, a dimly burning wick, he will not be quenched.
　　　　　Unto the peoples right orders shall he bring forth.

4　　He shall not be extinguished, nor shall he be crushed
　　　Until he shall have set right order in the earth.
　　　　Yea, for his revelation the Isles do wait.

CHORUS

42:5 So declareth God, the Lord,
　　　　He who created the heavens and stretched them out,
　　　　　Who spread out the earth and that which springs
　　　　　　　　　　　　　　　　　　　forth from it;
　　　Who giveth life to mankind upon it
　　　And spirit to those who walk thereon.

GOD ADDRESSES THE SERVANT

42:6 I, God, have called thee in truth,
　　　　And I hold fast thy hand and I guard thee;

---

[7] Julian Morgenstern, *Some Significant Antecedents of Christianity* (E. J. Brill, Leiden, 1966), pp. 41–60, used with permission.

And I give thee as a covenant of the people,
    As a light of the nations do I set thee,
7   To open the blind eyes,
    To bring forth the prisoner from the dungeon,
      From the place of confinement those who sit in
                darkness.

THE SERVANT COMMUNES WITH HIMSELF

61:1   The spirit of my Lord, God, is upon me,
    Because the Lord has anointed me.
To bring good tidings unto the afflicted hath He sent me;
    To bind up those broken of heart,
To proclaim freedom unto the captives
    And the opening of fetters unto those who are bound;
49:9a   To say to those who are confined, Come forth,
    To those who are in darkness, Show yourselves.
61:10   I will greatly rejoice in the Lord,
    My soul shall exult in my God;
For he hath clothed me in raiment of salvation,
    With the robe of vindication hath he covered me.
As the bridegroom binds on an ornament,
    And as the bride adorns herself with her jewels. . . .[8]

THE SERVANT SPEAKS

49:1   Hearken, ye Isles, unto me,
    And listen, ye peoples afar off.
The Lord hath called me from the womb,
    From my mother's loins He pronounced my name.
2   And he made my mouth like a sharp sword;
    In the shadow of His hand He concealed me.
Yea, He made me a polished arrow;
    In His quiver He hid me away.

[8] Here quite certainly a half-verse, consisting of a double distich, has been lost from the original text.

3   And He said to me, My servant art thou,
       O Israel, through whom I shall be glorified.

4   But I thought, in vain have I toiled,
       For naught and vanity have I spent my strength.
    Yet surely my case rests with the Lord;
       Yea, my recompense is with my God.

5c   And I was esteemed in the eyes of the Lord;
       Yea, my God has been my helper.

5ab   But now sayeth the Lord,
       He who formed me from the womb to be His servant,
    To bring back Jacob unto Him,
       And that Israel might be regathered unto Him;

6   Yea, He sayeth: It is too light a thing that thou shouldst
                         be a servant unto Me
    In order to raise up the tribes of Jacob
       And to bring back the scattered ones of Israel;
    So I have appointed thee as the light of the nations,
       In order that My salvation may reach to the end of
                                 the earth.

CHORUS

50:10   Whoever among you is a fearer of the Lord
       Let him hearken to the voice of His servant.
    Whoever is one who walks in darkness,
       So that he has no light,
    Let him put his trust in the name of the Lord,
       And let him lean upon his God.

THE SERVANT SPEAKS

50:4   My Lord, God, hath given unto me
       The tongue of experts to know how
          To give answer unto blasphemers.
    Day by day He stirs up for me
       An ear to hearken, as do disciples.

5   My Lord, God, hath opened for me (my) ear, .
      And I did not rebel;
        Backwards I did not turn.

6   My back I gave to smiters
      And my cheeks to those who plucked (my beard).
      My face I did not hide
        From shame and spittle.

7   But my Lord, God, was a helper unto me;
      Therefore I did not let myself feel humiliated.
      Therefore I set my face like a flint,
        For I knew that I would not be put to shame.

8-9a Close at hand is my Vindicator; who then would prove
                              me in the wrong?
      Whoever would enter into litigation with me, let us
                              stand up together;
      Whoever would have a case at law against me, let
                              him draw nigh to me.

CHORUS

52:13 Behold, the servant of the Lord hangs suspended;
      He is raised aloft and lifted up and is very high.

14   Even while the masses gazed upon him with amazement
      His appearance was marred beyond human sem-
                              blance,
      And his form beyond that of the sons of men.

15   Thus many nations kept staring at him;
      At him kings clenched their mouths;
      For something never told them before they were
                              beholding,
      And something unheard of they were pondering over.

THE CHORUS SPEAKS IN THE ROLE OF THE PEOPLES

53:1   Who has put faith in our report,
      And the power of God, to whom has it revealed itself?

2   For he grew up like a suckling plant before us,
         Yea, even as a root out of arid soil.
       He had neither form nor comeliness, that we should take
                                         notice of him,
         Nor had he stateliness, that we should hold him in
                                              esteem.

3   Despised, yea, lowliest of men,
         A man of affliction and acquainted with disease;
       Yea, even as one who hides his face from us;
         So we despised him and esteemed him not.

4   But actually our sicknesses was he carrying,
         Yea, our afflictions he was bearing himself.
       But we regarded him as plagued,
         Striken by God and afflicted.

5   But he was pierced because of our transgressions,
         Crushed because of our iniquities
       Chastisement for our well-being was upon him,
         And through his wounds there was healing for us.

6   We all like sheep have gone astray,
         Each one in his own way have we turned.
       But the Lord has imposed upon him
         The iniquity of us all.

7   He was oppressed and humiliated,
         Yet he would not open his mouth,
       As a lamb that is led to slaughter,
         Yea, even as a sheep before its shearers remains dumb.

8   From confinement and from judgment was he taken.
         And as for his generation, who can blame it,
       That he was cut off from the land of life,
         Because of our transgressions he was plague-stricken
                                          unto death?

9   And his grave was set among the wicked,
         Yea, with the doers of evil he lay in his death,
       Even though he had committed no crime,
         Nor was deceit found in his mouth.

10   But the Lord willed to crush him, so He let him be
                                                      pierced.
        In truth he has given himself as a guilt-offering.
        But he shall see posterity which will endure for long.
        So the purpose of the Lord shall prosper by his hand.

GOD IS THE SPEAKER

53:11   Through his personal suffering he shall bring salvation
                                                          nigh:
        Through his own tragedy shall My servant bring
                                       vindication to the masses,
            While their iniquity he will bear.
12   Therefore will I assign to him a portion among the
                                                        masses,
        And the mighty ones shall he divide as spoil,
        In exchange for having exposed himself to death
            And having let himself be reckoned with transgres-
                                                          sors.
        Yea, the sin of the masses has he borne,
            And for transgressors has he made supplication.

It is exceedingly interesting that in these Servant Songs
there are two points at which the prophet reported Yahweh
as saying that the Servant actually is a covenant; he does
not merely make or renew a covenant, but he actually is
the covenant himself.

        I am the Lord, I have called you in righteousness,
            I have taken you by the hand and kept you;
        I have given you as a covenant to the people,
            a light to the nations (Is. 42:6; cf. Lk. 2:32).

        Thus says the Lord:
        "In a time of favor I have answered you,
            in a day of salvation I have helped you;

> I have kept you and given you
> as a covenant to the people" (Is. 49:8).

Jesus, therefore, as he began his mission from the Father was the personification, the reality, of Yahweh's covenant and all the love and faithful grace-bearing qualities which comprise that covenant. There is surely a Hebraic background to St. John's Prologue.

And the Word became flesh and dwelt among us, full of grace and truth (Jn. 1:14).

For the law was given through Moses; grace and truth came through Jesus Christ (Jn. 1:17).

God's word or pledge to Abraham was now in human form, and at his baptism Jesus began to enter into his passion. "Baptism" in the Red Sea and the symbol itself of baptism have a close connection with suffering; the candidate descends into the depths of the dark waters and comes up into the world of light—the symbolism betokens life through death. Jesus himself said,

I have a baptism to be baptized with; and how I am constrained until it is accomplished! (Lk. 12:50).

The baptism of Jesus looked forward to his passion, and therefore it is wholly pertinent that he should have been manifested as the Servant of the Lord at the Jordan.

Jesus' baptism, as an earnest of his passion and in which he appears as the covenant personified, draws together many theological aspects of the former covenants. For example, 1 Peter 3:18–22 associated the passion of Jesus, the deluge and covenant with Noah, and the baptism of Christians.

For Christ also died for sins once for all, the righteous for the
unrighteous, that he might bring us to God, being put to death in
the flesh but made alive in the spirit: in which he went and
preached to the spirits in prison, who formerly did not obey,
when God's patience waited in the days of Noah, during the
building of the ark, in which a few, that is, eight persons, were
saved through water. Baptism, which corresponds to this, now
saves you, not as a removal of dirt from the body but as an appeal
to God for a clear conscience, through the resurrection of Jesus
Christ, who has gone into heaven and is at the right hand of God,
with angels, authorities, and powers subject to him.

St. Paul saw baptism as the fulfillment of the circumcision
covenant with Abraham.

In him also you were circumcised with a circumcision made without hands, by putting off the body of flesh in the circumcision of
Christ; and you were buried with him in baptism, in which you
were also raised with him through faith in the working of God,
who raised him from the dead (Col. 2:11–12).

The gift of the Spirit in baptism can be seen as the
plenitude of God's former favor on Mount Sinai; for example,
in Ephesians 1:13–14 we read,

In him you also, who have heard the word of truth, the gospel of
your salvation, and have believed in him, were sealed with the
promised Holy Spirit, which is the guarantee of our inheritance
until we acquire possession of it, to the praise of his glory.

However, it seemed necessary that Jesus should undergo
this baptism first through the hands of John that he might
fulfill all the prophecies concerning salvation. Jesus' first
suffering came immediately after his baptism, when, like
the Israelites, he was driven into the wilderness.

THE TEMPTATIONS

Jesus' mission from the Father appeared to begin with his baptism by John in the Jordan, an event which we have suggested would recall to the people not only Israel's crossing of the Jordan into the Promised Land but also her crossing of the Red Sea into the wilderness of Sinai on her pilgrimage to the Promised Land.

Jesus, summing up in himself the whole corporate personality of Israel, was led immediately after his baptism into the wilderness by the Spirit.[9] St. Mark reports merely,

The Spirit immediately drove him out into the wilderness. And he was in the wilderness forty days, tempted by Satan; and he was with the wild beasts; and the angels ministered to him (Mk. 1:12–13).

Some scholars have thought that this recalls to some extent the temptation of Adam. St. Matthew and St. Luke, however, give a fuller description of Jesus' temptation. They each list the three same temptations, but in a different order.

In St. Matthew's account we cannot help being reminded of Moses. Indeed, Matthew with his fondness for portraying Jesus as the second Moses may have added details in order to paint Jesus in this light. In Matthew, Jesus fasts forty days and forty nights as did Moses on Mount Sinai before he received the ten commandments (Ex. 24:18). In Luke, Jesus fasts "forty days" but possibly we are meant to infer that he fasted at night as well.[10] In any event, Jesus' temptations recall those of Israel in the wilderness.

[9] Corporate personality has a "business economy" ring, but it is difficult to find another suitable term.

[10] But, on the other hand, there may have been a difference, for in some religions fasting lasts from sunrise to sunset but the devotees partake of food and drink during the night.

The first temptation, both in Matthew and Luke, was concerned with the satisfaction of Jesus' hunger. The tempter
addressed him as the Son of God and bade him make the
stones into bread. Jesus refused and in his answer quoted
scripture:

It is written, "Man shall not live by bread alone, but by every
word that proceeds from the mouth of God" (Mt. 4:4).

Jesus quoted directly from Deuteronomy 8:3b, which is a
section about the temptation of hunger which the children
of Israel experienced in the wilderness and the gift of manna
which God bestowed on them. The whole verse reads:

And he [God] humbled you and let you hunger and fed you with
manna, which you did not know, nor did your fathers know; that
he might make you know that man does not live by bread alone,
but that man lives by everything that proceeds out of the mouth
of the Lord (Deut. 8:3).

In the second temptation in Matthew the devil took Jesus
to the holy city and set him on the outer wall (pinnacle),
which runs round the edge of the sheer rock upon which the
Temple in Jerusalem was built. Josephus[11] said that standing
on the rock made one quite giddy. Indeed, one looked down
almost at right angles into the Kedron valley and the graves
dotted around its edges. Jesus was asked to perform a wonder
feat which apparently was without much theological significance. He met the temptation by quoting from Deuteronomy 6:16.

You shall not tempt the Lord your God (Mt. 4:7).

---

[11] A Jewish historian approximately contemporary with Jesus.

Once more this quotation was concerned with the Israelites' experience in the wilderness. The Israelites tempted God when they wanted water at Massah (cf. 1 Cor. 10).

The third temptation in Matthew involved the devil's offering to Christ the kingdoms of the world. Jesus again replied by quoting from Deuteronomy 6:13.

You shall worship the Lord your God, and him only shall you serve (Mt. 4:10).

This probably refers to the incident of the golden calf and the Israelites' idolatry on that occasion (Ex. 32).

We do not know how the evangelists became informed about the temptations of Jesus save that he must have told them. Even if the quotations, which they placed in Jesus' mouth, were the reflection of the Christian community after the resurrection of Jesus, nevertheless the narrative recorded by the three synoptic gospels enables us to see the importance of the temptation-event to Jesus and the early community.

Jesus was seen as the corporate Israel, the king or prophet suffering on behalf of his people. But his idea of kingship or Messiahship was different from that generally expected among the Jews contemporary with him. The temptations revealed Jesus rejecting a Messiahship which would have included anything of the spectacular. Tradition spoke of economic and agricultural prosperity at the coming of the Messiah, perhaps even the return of manna for the people. But Jesus refused to turn a few stones into bread for his own benefit; later, however, he multiplied the loaves in order both to satisfy the hunger of those who followed him and to reveal to them a little more of his person. Jesus refused to throw himself down from the pinnacle of the

Temple and thereby declined to accommodate himself to a popular belief that the Messiah would appear in that place and announce victory. Jesus rejected the earthly kingdoms, for his kingdom is "not of this world." Jesus emerged victorious from his conflict with the devil, and his consciousness of his mission as the Suffering Servant rather than as the political Messiah was fully confirmed.[12]

Jesus then began his mission and worked around the Sea of Galilee among the businessmen prospering on the salt trade from the Dead Sea, a trade which enabled them to conduct a flourishing fish industry. Josephus tells us that there were fifteen cities around the Sea of Galilee, and these are now being rediscovered by underwater excavations. Matthew saw Jesus' work in the rich and fertile land of the tribes of Zebulun and Naphtali, among the large land estates (latifundia) often possessed by foreign, non-Jewish, or half-Jewish landlords, as a fulfillment of one more text in Isaiah.

> The land of Zebulun and the land of Naphtali,
> toward the sea, across the Jordan,
> Galilee of the Gentiles—
> the people who sat in darkness
> have seen a great light,
> and for those who sat in the region and shadow of death
> light has dawned (Mt. 4:15–16; cf. Is. 9:1–2).

---

[12] Jesus seems to be like the prophets who, as we have seen, were sometimes obliged to reject the political and earthly ambitions of the leaders of the State. One wonders whether Jesus could have remained politically indifferent to the contemporary situation. He appears to have been more sympathetic to the pacifists than to the Zealots. However, his prophetic character lies in his work for the kingdom of heaven rather than the kingdom of the earth.

FURTHER READING

Davies, W. D., *The Setting of the Sermon on the Mount.* Cambridge University Press, New York, 1964.

Dupont, Jacques, "Les Tentations de Jésus dans le Recit de Luc." *Sciences Ecclésiastiques* 14 (1962), pp. 7-29.

Engell, I., *Studies in Divine Kingship in the Ancient Near East.* Almqvist and Wiksells, Uppsala, 1943.

Feuillet, André, "Le Baptême de Jésus." *Revue Biblique* 71 (1964), pp. 321-352.

Kraeling, C. H., *John the Baptist.* Scribner, New York, 1951.

Mowinckel, S., *He that Cometh.* Abingdon, New York and Nashville, 1956.

Steinmann, J., *St. Jean-Baptiste et la Spiritualité du Désert.* Editions du Seuil, Paris, 1955.

14 Jesus and the New Torah

Behold the days are coming, says the Lord, when I will make a new covenant with the house of Israel and the house of Judah, not like the covenant which I made with their fathers when I took them by the hand to bring them out of the land of Egypt, my covenant which they broke, though I was their husband, says the Lord. But this is the covenant which I will make with the house of Israel after those days, says the Lord: I will put my law within them, and I will write it upon their hearts; and I will be their God, and they shall be my people. And no longer shall each man teach his neighbor and each his brother, saying, "Know the Lord," for they shall all know me, from the least of them to the greatest, says the Lord; for I will forgive their iniquity, and I will remember their sin no more (Jer. 31:31–34).

If, as has been thought, the author of St. Matthew's Gospel wished to present Jesus as the second Moses, the expected prophet of Deuteronomy 18:15, then, perhaps, we can see another indication of this in the Sermon on the Mount. St. Matthew seems to have collected together certain portions or summaries of Jesus' teaching and to have presented them as though Jesus had delivered them in one Sermon on a "Mount," as, in a similar way, the author of Exodus had presented Moses giving the decalogue and the Book of the Covenant on Mount Sinai, although it was not possible that all those laws were promulgated at that time.

St. Luke places Jesus' Sermon on a plain and gives a shorter version of it. Matthew does not name the Mount on which Jesus delivered this discourse, but some have attempted to locate the place near the Sea of Galilee. A church has been built on the site determined by early tradition.

The Sermon falls roughly into the following parts:

1. the beatitudes;
2. the parables[1] about salt and light;
3. the words of Jesus on the law (murder, adultery, divorce, swearing, retaliation, love of one's enemies);
4. almsgiving, prayer (including the Lord's Prayer), fasting;
5. Jesus' words on treasures, the sound eye, on serving two masters, on anxiety, judging, profaning the holy, God's answer to prayer, the golden rule, the narrow gate, the test of a good person, deception, hearers and doers of the word.

THE AUDIENCE

We cannot know precisely before what type of audience Jesus was speaking, for such a variety of subjects cannot have been the matter for only one discourse. However, it would seem that the author of the Gospel of Matthew may have had a more precise audience in mind or might even have composed the discourse to deliver on a special feast day. In the Gospels Jesus is shown delivering the discourse to the crowds (in Matthew) and to the disciples (in Luke). Professor J. Jeremias in his brilliant work on the Sermon on the Mount has suggested that the Sermon is designed for the

[1] See pp. 175 f. for definition of parable.

scholars or scribes in the first part, for the pious Jewish laymen in the second (the Pharisees), and for the Christians in the third.[2] Professor Krister Stendahl sees Matthew's Gospel as a product of a school for teachers and leaders in the early Church.[3] The present author[4] has suggested that this Sermon may have been delivered in the Syrian Christian Church during the ten day period of repentance practiced between New Year's Day and the Day of Atonement, when all classes of people would be examining their consciences about the duties of their station, confessing their sins, and forming resolutions for the future.

Whichever theory is correct, we can be sure that this Sermon is of composite character and designed for a wider audience than the twelve disciples. The literary structure is a good example of the Jewish manner of teaching; in short, the Sermon has rhythmic sentences and is easily memorized.[5] Professor Burney and others have noted the poetic structure of many of the parts; for example,

> *Luke 6:27–28—Matthew 5:44*
> Love your enemies
> Do good to your haters,
> Bless your cursers,
> Pray for your persecutors.

> *Matthew 5:45*
> He causeth His sun to rise upon evil and good,
> And raineth upon just and unjust.

[2] J. Jeremias, *The Sermon on the Mount*, trans. by N. Perrin (Oxford University Press, New York, 1961).

[3] K. Stendahl, *The School of Matthew* (Almqvist and Wiksells, Uppsala, 1954).

[4] "Yom Kippur and the Matthaean form of the Pater Noster," *Worship* (December, 1967), pp. 609–619.

[5] See, for example, B. Gerhardsson, *Memory and Manuscript* (Uppsala, 1967), pp. 71–181.

Luke 12:22–23—Matthew 6:25

Be not anxious for your life, what ye shall eat,
Neither for your body, what ye shall put on:
Is not the life more than meat?
And the body than raiment?

Matthew 7:7–8—Luke 11:9–10

Ask, and it shall be given you;
Seek, and ye shall find;
Knock and it shall be opened to you.
For every asker receiveth;
And the seeker findeth;
And to the knocker it shall be opened.[6]

Dr. Austen Farrer has seen an even more intricate literary plan in the Sermon and has suggested that the whole Sermon falls into two parts: the beatitudes and then the rest. These two parts he compares to the ten commandments (the decalogue) and the Book of the Covenant. He suggests that just as the Book of the Covenant is a commentary or a more detailed application of the decalogue, so the Sermon on the Mount is a commentary on the beatitudes. This theory is not without its attractions.

THE BEATITUDES

The decalogue is mainly apodictic law, that is, a "Thou shalt not" form of law. Jesus came, not with a negative law and a curse for its infringement, but with a positive law and a blessing. The beatitudes express the positive qualities needed by the citizens of the kingdom of heaven. One notices that whereas St. Luke has treated them as purely "social conditions," St. Matthew has raised them to a spiritual level.

[6] C. F. Burney, *Poetry of Our Lord* (Oxford, 1925) p. 67.

This is readily discernible by placing them in parallel columns:

INTRODUCTION

Matthew 5:1–2

1 Seeing the crowds, he went up on the mountain, and when he sat down his disciples came to him. 2 And he opened his mouth and taught them, saying:

Luke 6:12, 20

12 In these days he went out into the hills to pray; and all night he continued in prayer to God. 20 And he lifted up his eyes on his disciples, and said:

THE BEATITUDES

Matthew 5:3–12

3 "Blessed are the poor in spirit, for theirs is the kingdom of heaven.

4 "Blessed are those who mourn, for they shall be comforted.

5 "Blessed are the meek, for they shall inherit the earth.

6 "Blessed are those who hunger and thirst for righteousness, for they shall be satisfied.

7 "Blessed are the merciful, for they shall obtain mercy.

8 "Blessed are the pure in heart, for they shall see God.

9 "Blessed are the peacemakers, for they shall be called sons of God.

10 "Blessed are those who are persecuted for righteousness' sake, for theirs is the kingdom of heaven.

Luke 6:20–23

20 "Blessed are you poor, for yours is the kingdom of God.

21 "Blessed are you that hunger now, for you shall be satisfied. Blessed are you that weep now, for you shall laugh.

11 "Blessed are you when men revile you and persecute you and utter all kinds of evil against you falsely on my account.

22 "Blessed are you when men hate you, and when they exclude you and revile you and cast out your name as evil, on account of the Son of man!

12 "Rejoice and be glad, for your reward is great in heaven, for so men persecuted the prophets who were before you."

23 "Rejoice in that day, and leap for joy, for behold, your reward is great in heaven; for so their fathers did to the prophets."

In these beatitudes Jesus presents the highest teaching of Judaism.[7]

On poverty:

He who is poor in this world will be rich in the World-to-Come (*Alphabeth of R. Akiba*, 22; edit. Jellineck; Talmud).[8]

God searched for the best gift He might offer Israel, and He found nothing better than poverty (*Hagigah*, 9).

On meekness:

Hillel said: My humiliation is my exaltation; my exaltation is my humiliation.

The Talmud says: Those who are humiliated but humiliate not, those who hear themselves shamed but do not answer, who act out of love and rejoice in their sufferings (*Shabbat* 88b).

On mercy:

Be careful that you withhold not pity, for he who withholds pity from his fellow man is likened by Scripture to a worshipper of idols, and he throws off the yoke of the heaven (Talmud).[9]

---

[7] See also D. Flusser, "Blessed are the Poor in Spirit," *Israel Exploration Journal* 10 (1960), pp. 1–13, where the author compares the beatitudes to certain parts of the Dead Sea Scrolls.

[8] Reprinted from *The Talmudic Anthology* by Louis I. Newman (Behrman House, Inc., 1261 Broadway, New York, N. Y.).

[9] *Ibid.*

On purity of heart:

The Rabbis used to say: As the spirit was given to thee pure, so return it pure (*Shabbat* 152b).

On peace:

Hillel said: Be of the disciples of Aaron, loving peace and pursuing peace, loving thy fellow-creatures, and drawing them near to the Torah (*Aboth*, 1, 12).[10]

On persecution:

Rabbi Hanina b. Papa said: Because the Israelites surrender their lives for the Torah and the sanctification of the Name, God makes them a blessing in the world (Talmud).[11]

Indeed, the rabbis taught that the *Shekinah* (or the Glorious Presence of God) can dwell, not where there is sadness, but only where there is joy. They also taught that one must acquire certain virtues, namely, zeal, integrity, purity, holiness, humility, and fear of sin, before one is given the gift of the Shekinah, called in extra-biblical works the Holy Spirit. The blessedness of the Christians consists precisely in the possession of the Holy Spirit.

THE SALT AND THE LIGHT

It is precisely because of the possession of these qualities listed in the preceding section that Christians can be said to be the salt of the earth and the light of the world. These two parables of Christ throw into greater relief the character of the Christian in the world.

---

[10] C. G. Montefiore and H. Loewe, eds., *A Rabbinic Anthology* (Harper [Torchbooks], New York, 1963). Used with permission of World Publishing Company, Cleveland, Ohio.

[11] Newman, *op. cit.*

You are the salt of the earth; but if salt has lost its taste, how shall its saltness be restored? It is no longer good for anything except to be thrown out and trodden under foot by men (Mt. 5:13–16).

This synonym might have been especially striking to people living in Palestine. There were two kinds of salt in Palestine, that which was evaporated from the sea and did not lose its savor and that which was found in ridges and salt hills, especially those within the vicinity of the Dead Sea. Indeed, today by the Dead Sea there is a long ridge, nine miles long, of salt hills, one of which is called Lot's wife. Such salt can easily lose its savor by becoming mixed with dust or gypsum. It is the kind of salt which is used as a fertilizer for soil.

Hence, this parable depicts the Christians as the fertilizer of the soil in which the word of God is to grow. If they themselves do not perform their function, then they are not even good for themselves and are thrown out. Such salt of the soil can be put on the flat roofs of houses and trodden under the feet of men and women and so strengthen the floor of the house, but in this case it has lost its peculiar function as salt.[12] Thus, if the disciples were the salt of the earth, they would be the means of producing good seed in the earth.

> For as the rain and the snow come down from heaven,
>   and return not thither but water the earth,
>   making it bring forth and sprout,
>   giving seed to the sower and bread to the eater,
>   so shall my word be that goes forth from my mouth;
>   it shall not return to me empty,

[12] E. P. Deatrick, "Salt, Soil, Savor," *Biblical Archaeologist* 25 (1962), pp. 41–48.

but it shall accomplish that which I purpose,
   and prosper in the thing for which I sent it (Is. 55:10–11).

The simile of salt was also used by the Jewish teachers as a synonym for the Torah or law of Israel. So the disciples and Christians are depicted as living *toroth* (plural of Torah), just as the Jewish teachers, who taught and lived the law well, were thought of as living embodiments of the law. One can compare with this concept a nun or monk who is said to be a living Rule, or people who are the epitomes or paradigms of certain virtues. Thus, the expression to "eat the salt of man" meant to derive sustenance from him.

In Leviticus 2:13 we find a reference to the "salt of the covenant." This may have applied to the salt which was sprinkled on offerings, but it was also used in a symbolic sense. Particularly holy and inviolable obligations were designated as "salt covenants" (Num. 18:19; 2 Chron. 13:5), for salt was the symbol of the eternal duration of such covenants. Therefore, salt was a potent symbol of the covenant between God and Israel. The Jewish teachers taught that just as the world could not do without salt, neither could it do without the Torah (*Soferim* 15:8).

Thus, when Jesus denoted his followers as the salt of the soil or the earth, he was transferring the efficacy of the Torah of Israel to them as living *toroth* and expressions of the Father and Son's covenant. Because the Servant of the Lord is a covenant to the people, so too the disciples must be a like covenant: the world is to derive sustenance from them, for they are to be the direct media of the covenant of God.

When Jesus compared them to light, he was using another symbol of the Torah. Wisdom, which was almost identified with the Torah by the time of Jesus, and the Shekinah were symbolized by light, the symbol of life and joy. It was said that the righteous men and women would shine like the light of the sun and the stars in the world to come. Jesus had called himself the light of the world (Jn. 8). Therefore, once again Matthew's Sermon pointed out the transmission of the character and function of Jesus to his followers.

JESUS' WORDS ON THE LAW

The words of Jesus on the law follow naturally these two parables. Jesus said that he had not come to abolish the law but to fulfill it. He demanded not less than the first Torah, but more. The men and women who most perfectly fulfill and teach Jesus' commandments will be the greatest in the kingdom of heaven. When Jesus said, "Unless your righteousness exceeds that of the scribes and Pharisees, you will never enter the kingdom of heaven" (Mt. 5:20), he was, indeed, affirming that the scribes and Pharisees had righteousnesss but did not have it fully. Jesus appeared to demand very high qualities for entrance into the kingdom of heaven.

From this point the Sermon passes smoothly into the next section which discusses six points of the Jewish law and shows how they are to be fulfilled even more perfectly than in the old dispensation. Here Jesus used the accustomed methodology of the Jewish teachers.[13] He stated the law and then gave the deeper interpretation. The first person singular (I) does not necessarily refer only to Jesus, but Jesus used this format as an authorized expositor of the Jewish law would do. Jesus chose to comment on the three sins most abominated by his Jewish brothers and sisters.

[13] See David Daube, *The New Testament and Rabbinic Judaism* (Athlone Press, London, 1956), pp. 52–62.

First, he spoke of *murder*. Jesus taught that even anger
and insulting words break the commandment "Thou shalt
not kill." This was common rabbinic teaching; for example,
the statement "Thou shalt not murder" means:

Thou shalt not cause thy brother's blood to boil with bitterness
because of thine actions (*Pesikta Rabbati,* 25:1).[14]

However, when Jesus gave this teaching, it may have been
especially appropriate because of the bitter disputes between
the two divisions among the Pharisees. There was the strict
school of Pharisees (the School of Shammai) and the more
lenient school (the School of Hillel). The Sadducees tended
to support the stricter school, which appears to have been
inclined toward Jewish nationalism, while the School of
Hillel was more pacifist. Disputes over ritual and academic
questions, such as handwashing or the way to offer sacrifice,
arose in the academies and reached such a pitch that abusive
words and even acts of violence were sometimes committed.
But Jesus demanded perfect respect for the dignity of the
human person and his individual views.

The following quotation summarizes some of the differences between the two schools:

The words of both schools are the words of the living God, but
the law follows the rulings of the School of Hillel because the
Hillelites were gentle and modest, and studied both their own
opinions and the opinions of the other school, and humbly mentioned the words of the other school before theirs. The preference
accorded to the School of Hillel teach you that he who humbles
himself the Lord raises up, and he who exalts himself the Lord
humbles; greatness flees him who seeks greatness; greatness may

[14] Newman, *op. cit.*

follow him who flees from greatness; he who [impatiently] tries to force time, is thrown back by time; he who [patiently] yields to time, finds time standing by him (*Erubin* 13b).

Matthew 5:23 is particularly arresting because the gentle Hillel was nearly lynched when he came to offer a gift at the altar. His friends barely rescued him from the hands of the strict Shammaites. We probably have another reference to the murder of a lenient Pharisee in Matthew 23:35; that verse refers to "the blood of Zechariah the son of Barachiah, whom you [the Pharisees] murdered between the sanctuary and the altar."

Jesus recommended that an understanding between the accused and the accuser be reached on the way to the court (probably the *Beth din,* the Jewish local assembly) which decided religious and other questions. St. Matthew in this part of the Sermon uses many more Jewish terms than does St. Luke in the parallel passage.[15]

Jesus then passed on to the subject of *adultery* or *unchastity*. Jesus demanded purity from the heart, a virtue insisted upon by the holy Pharisees. It was said that the term *Kiddushin,* denoting "sanctification," was used of marriage because

the husband prohibits his wife to the whole world like an object which is dedicated to the Sanctuary (*Kiddushin* 2b).

Both parties were bound to strict chastity, and the proverb ran,

Immorality in the house is like a worm on vegetables (*Sotah* 3b).

---

[15] This background to Jewish teaching would support Professor Jeremias' thesis that this first part of the Sermon is directed towards the scholars.

On the other hand, the presence of God dwelt especially with chaste married people.

> When a husband and wife are worthy, the *Shechinah* is with them; when they are not worthy fire consumes them (*Sotah* 17a).

Jesus used hyperboles to emphasize his points. He spoke against self-abuse (Mt. 5:30) as well as impurity with another person.

St. Matthew's version of Jesus' teaching on *divorce* has proved a difficulty to some people. In Mark 10:11–12 and Luke 16:18 Jesus is presented with a choice between the Shammai view of marriage and divorce and that of Hillel's School. Jesus took a stricter view than either. He forbade divorce absolutely. In St. Matthew's version, however, the clause "except on the ground of unchastity" is added. Some scholars have thought that this was an exception, but many now agree that the Greek word for unchastity (*porneia*) in this context probably means "incest" or forbidden relationships. This meaning of *porneia* is probably found in 1 Corinthians 5:1 and Acts 15:20. If this meaning is correct, then Jesus only allowed divorce (for betrothal and marriage) when the union had been incestuous according to Jewish law.

Jesus teaching on *swearing* may be connected with the section on murder. Oaths usually were taken by a defendant and were in the nature of a repudiation of the claims of the accuser, although in Mishnaic[16] times the oath was sometimes taken by a plaintiff. The juror swore in the name of Yahweh and held in his hand a bible or sacred object. But the oath was employed only for want of better evidence; if

---

[16] Approximately third century A.D.

there were witnesses, their evidence was accepted as full legal evidence, and it was considered one's duty to speak the truth whether with or without an oath. The general principle was "Let thy 'yea' be 'yea' and thy 'nay' be 'nay'" (B.M. 49a; cf. Mt. 5:37 and Jas. 5:12). The Essenes[17] avoided swearing altogether and deemed it worse than perjury: "He that cannot be believed without an oath is already condemned" (Josephus, *The Jewish War*, 2:8, 6). Philo[18] said, "The bare word of a virtuous man should be like an oath, steadfast, inviolable, and true. Should necessity absolutely require an oath let a man swear by his father and mother . . . instead of by the name of the highest and first Essence [God]."

In the same way Jesus required of his followers absolute truthfulness and integrity so that there would be no need to swear. Not only did Jesus forbid swearing by the name of God himself but also even by the holy places.

Concerning *retaliation* Jesus appeared to have taken a kind of pacifist attitude. The Pharisees themselves had modified the *lex talionis* (law of exact retribution) found in Exodus 21:24; Deuteronomy 19:21, and Leviticus 24:20. Indeed, they suggested monetary compensation instead of a *quid pro quo*. Some of the noblest sentiments are found among the rabbinic teachings concerning returning good for evil, for example,

They who are oppressed and oppress not, who listen to insults without retorting, who act lovingly and are happy under trials, of them it is written, "Let them who love Him be as the sun when it goeth forth in its might [Judg. 5:31]" (*Shabboth* 88b).

17 A sect of strict Jews.
18 A Jewish-Alexandrian philosopher approximately contemporary with Jesus.

Who is mighty? He who turns an enemy into his friend (*Aboth Rabbi Nathan* 23).[19]

Once again Jesus' teaching at this point is best understood against the background of the Pharisaic quarrels and the aggressiveness of the Zealots. In Matthew 5:39–47 Jesus demanded, as it were, supererogatory works. In the Old Testament (Ex. 22:26) the law required a man not to take a cloak overnight as a pledge; Jesus, on the other hand, counseled his disciples to give away even this. Matthew 5:41 might be explained by the practice of the Roman soldiers which demanded that the men carry their equipment one mile. But there is also the example of Hillel's loving kindness:

There was a man of a wealthy family who had become poor. Hillel provided him with a horse to ride upon and with a servant to run before him for three miles (*Kethubot* 67b).

Jesus' demands were invitations to infinite generosity on the part of his followers (*compare* Heb. 11:35–40).

Matthew 5:43–48 may expand Jesus' teaching on non-violence, *on loving one's enemies*. Formerly, scholars could not find a citation concerning hating one's enemies, but in the Dead Sea Scrolls literature we do read some suggestion of this, though the hatred seems to be against evil rather than evil men. In fact, aspirations similar to Jesus' teaching are found in the Hymn of the Initiants:

> I will heap no evil on any,
>   but pursue all men with good,
>   knowing that only with God

---

[19] Judah Goldin, trans., *The Fathers according to Rabbi Nathan* (Yale University Press, New Haven, 1955).

lies the judgment of all living,
and He it is who will award each man his deserts.
I will not be envious
of the profit of wickedness;
for wealth unrighteously gotten my soul shall not lust. . . .
I will harbour no angry grudge
against those that indeed repent,
but neither will I show compassion
to any that turn from the way. . . .[20]

Both the writer of this hymn and Jesus spoke in violent times.

Jesus brought to a close his exhortations to complete self-lessness with the words, "You, therefore, must be perfect, as your heavenly Father is perfect" (Mt. 5:48). St. Luke's version reads, "Be merciful, even as your Father is merciful" (6:36).

DUTIES OF PIETY

Jesus turned to *almsgiving,* probably (as Professor Jeremias suggests), addressing the pious laymen. Almsgiving was greatly stressed and reverenced by the Pharisees. Concerning this practice they said,

He who does charity and justice is as if he had filled the whole world with kindness (*Sukkah,* 49).

Charity knows neither race nor creed (*Gittin,* 61a).

Mar Ukba was accustomed to throw four zuzim every day in the hole of his neighbour's door, and walk away unseen. Once the poor recipient wished to know his benefactor, and ran out of his home to detect him, but he was too late (*Kethubot,* 67).

[20] Gaster, *op. cit.,* 129.

Thus, Jesus was reinforcing the rabbinical teaching. We can conjecture that he and his disciples gave alms (cf. Jn. 13:29).

Likewise, Jesus followed the best Jewish manner of *prayer* (Mt. 6:5–8).

R. Judah said: Thus did R. Akiba conduct himself: if he prayed in public, he would hasten with his prayer lest it be a hardship upon the public; but, if he prayed alone, he would pray long with many bowings (Talmud).[21]

Jesus himself is known to have retired for prayer alone and also to have taken the disciples into "retreat."[22]

But perhaps the ultimate difference between Jesus' prayer teaching and that of the rabbis was his invitation to men to address God as their true Father. The example of Jesus' prayer is found in the Our Father, about which many excellent books and articles have been written. Suffice it to draw attention here to Professor Manson's remark that the best commentary on the Lord's Prayer is the life and passion of Jesus.

Joseph Blenkinsopp[23] has pointed out the affinity between the prayer of the Agony in the Garden and the Pater Noster. In both Jesus addressed God as Father; in both there was mention of "thy will be done"; and in both were words concerning temptation. John 14–17 brings Jesus' teaching concerning the Fatherhood of God and one's relationship to him in prayer to a brilliant climax; this discourse may have been delivered at the institution of the Eucharist.

---

[21] Newman, *op. cit.*

[22] "He who recites his prayer in a voice heard by others is of a nature unworthy of trust" (*Berakot*, 24).

[23] "Apropos of the Lord's Prayer," *Heythrop Journal* 3, 1 (1962), pp. 51–60.

Jesus turned his attention next to the pious work of *fasting*. He himself fasted during his temptations and said that his disciples would fast when the "bridegroom" had been taken away from them. Jesus counseled his listeners that, instead of following customs close to those observed by mourners,[24] when fasting they should appear as though they were going to a banquet with washed face and anointed head, that is, they should fast with joy. These instructions on fasting are not given by Mark and Luke.

HIS FINAL EXHORTATIONS

Matthew 6:19–21 on *treasures* seems as if it belongs more properly to Matthew 6:1–4 (concerning almsgiving). Moth and worm could corrupt treasure because wealth was often computed in garments. It is possible that Jesus had in mind especially the rich Sadducees and possibly the Shammaites,[25] who were especially wealthy and did not even scruple to gain benefits through their religious services. This may be confirmed by looking at the next section.

It is just possible that "eye" in Matthew 6:22 indicates the Sanhedrin, for in Hebrew the letter *ayin* (not in our alphabet) means eye and was used as a symbol for the number seventy, the number of members in the Sanhedrin. In one of the Jewish commentaries we find the following reflection:

Thine eyes are as doves: Thine eyes: these refer to the Sanhedrin who are the eyes of the congregation, as it is written, *If it be hid from the eyes of the congregation* (Num. 15:24). There are two

---

[24] Five things were forbidden in fasting: bathing and anointing, shaving, eating and drinking, wearing sandals, and marital relations.

[25] Luke 12:33–34 places this pericope in context of Jesus' warning against the leaven of the Pharisees and other teaching about riches.

hundred and forty-eight limbs in the human body, and they move only by the direction of the eyes. So Israel can do nothing without their Sanhedrin (*Canticle Rabbah*, I. 15).

In the Dead Sea Scrolls there is a text which is thought to read,

"Behold, I will set your stones in antimony, and lay your foundations with sapphires" (Is. 54:11). This refers to the fact that they have founded the deliberative council of the community out of priests and laity—a veritable congregation of God's elect—like a sapphire among gems.[26]

Jesus' Sermon (or Matthew's) may have been politically orientated when he spoke of *serving two masters* in Matthew 6:24.

No one can serve two masters; for either he will hate the one and love the other, or he will be devoted to the one and despise the other. You cannot serve God and mammon.

This text was especially relevant for the Sanhedrin—and, of course, for Judas Iscariot. Luke placed this saying after the parable of the unjust steward and reported that after Jesus had given this teaching, "The Pharisees, who were lovers of money, heard all this, and they scoffed at him" (Lk. 16:14).

After Jesus had given this negative counsel concerning riches, he turned to more positive advice, bidding the people to have no *anxiety* about material things. A quotation from Hillel the Elder is apposite here:

[26] Gaster, *op. cit.*, p. 235.

> The more flesh, the more worms;
> the more possessions, the more worry . . .
> the more maidservants, the more immorality;
> the more menservants, the more thieving.
> But the more Torah, the more life;
> the more study and contemplation, the more wisdom . . .
> the more charity, the more peace.[27]

Above everything else Jesus required his disciples to seek the kingdom of heaven. The rabbis also demanded similar renunciations for the sake of the Torah.

If a man does not show himself as cruel towards himself, to his children and his household as a raven [to its young], he does not succeed in acquiring Torah (*Leviticus Rabbah* 19:1).

Jesus reached the culmination of his Sermon by requesting abstinence from *judging* others, a fault which was easily discernible in the Shammaites. Jesus' sense of humor was revealed as he spoke of charity toward another—taking the log out of one's own eye before one takes the speck out of another's. On judging, the rabbis taught, for example, as follows:

He who judges his fellow-man on the side of merit is himself judged on the side of merit (*Shabbat*, 127).

. . . judge every man in the most favourable light (*Abot*, 1, 6).

In Matthew 7:7–11 Jesus encouraged men and women to

[27] Reprinted by permission of Schocken Books, Inc., New York, from *Hillel The Elder: The Emergence of Classical Judaism* by Nahum N. Glatzer. Copyright © 1956 by B'Nai B'rith Hillel Foundations, Inc.

ask with confidence from the Heavenly Father; this too is consonant with the Jewish prayer mentality.

If thou has prayed, and prayed yet again, it is already declared to thee that thy prayer is heard (*Midrah Tehillim*, 14, Talmud).[28]

He who prays with the community will have his prayer granted (*Berakot*, 8a).

If a man sees that he has prayed without answer, he should continue praying (*Berakot*, 32).

Then Jesus recited the positive form of the *Golden Rule* of Hillel. Hillel had said,

What is hateful to you, do not do to your neighbor; that is the whole Torah; the rest is commentary; go study.[29]

Jesus said,

So whatever you wish that men would do to you, do so to them; for this is the law and the prophets (Mt. 7:12).

The demands of Jesus are difficult to meet but his demands are higher than those of the Jewish law because he gives the grace to fulfill them. Nevertheless, the Jewish law and the Jewish oral traditions taught, for example, by Hillel and his school had paved the way for these demands of perfection.

Matthew 7:15–20 reemphasizes John the Baptist's message. Jesus' warning is probably understood more clearly in the light of the history of the early Church and the false

---

[28] Newman, *op. cit.*
[29] Glatzer, *op. cit.*

prophets who arose during that period. (Prophets are more
prominent in Matthew and in John than in Mark and in
Luke.) This passage teaches that the fate of everyone de-
pends on good works, so that Matthew 7:21–23 anticipates
Matthew 25:31–46.

In this Sermon Jesus implemented once again the work
of the prophets. Like the Old Testament prophets, Jesus
was necessarily opposed to the ruling parties, who have become distracted both by materialistic advantages and an
overliteral interpretation of the ritual law. Jesus as the
prophet par excellence appeared as the epitome of Torah,
that is, of instruction or revelation, a term which might well
replace the term "law" with its harsh and rigid connotations.

Matthew 7:24–27 concludes with the parable of the house
on the rock. One's mind recalls with regard to this parable
the Qumran establishment with its community center or
house on the rock near the Dead Sea. Whereas we must take
seriously those scholars who suggest that the Qumran community were Zealots, yet the Qumran people, at least in
. some stages of their sojourn in the wilderness, do seem to
have been removed from the political intrigues of the Shammaites and the Sadducees in Jerusalem. Their concentration
was on the deeper meaning of the Torah, on prayer, study,
scholarship, holiness of life, and true community, so that
their community center, both physically and spiritually, was
founded on a rock:

In the Council of the Community there shall be twelve men and
three Priests, perfectly versed in all that is revealed of the Law,
whose works shall be truth, righteousness, justice, loving-kindness,
and humility. They shall preserve the faith in the Land with
steadfastness and meekness and shall atone for sin by the practice
of justice and by suffering the sorrows of affliction. They shall

walk with all men according to the standard of truth and the rule of the time.

When these are in Israel, the Council of the Community shall be established in truth. It shall be an Everlasting Plantation, a House of Holiness for Israel, an Assembly of Supreme Holiness for Aaron. They shall be witnesses to the truth at the Judgement, and shall be the elect of Goodwill who shall atone for the Land and pay to the wicked their reward. It shall be that tried wall, the precious corner-stone, whose foundations shall neither rock nor sway in their place [Is. 28:16]. It shall be a Most Holy Dwelling for Aaron, with everlasting knowledge of the Covenant of justice, and shall offer up sweet fragrance. It shall be a House of Perfection and Truth in Israel that they may establish a Covenant according to the everlasting precepts.[30]

FURTHER READING

Daube, David, *The New Testament and Rabbinic Judaism.* Athlone Press, London, 1956, pp. 52-62.

Davies, W. D., *The Setting of the Sermon on the Mount.* Cambridge University Press, Cambridge, 1964, pp. 94 ff.

Farrer, A. M., *St. Matthew and St. Mark.* Dacre Press: Black, London, 1954.

Finkel, Asher, *The Pharisees and the Teacher of Nazareth.* E. J. Brill, Leiden, 1964.

Finkelstein, L., *Akiba: Scholar, Saint and Martyr.* Covici Friede, New York, 1936.

Jeremias, J., *The Sermon on the Mount,* trans. by N. Perrin. Oxford University Press, New York, 1961 (Fortress, Philadelphia, 1963, paperback).

Montefiore, C. G., and H. Loewe, eds., *A Rabbinic Anthology.* Harper (Torchbooks), New York, 1960.

[30] G. Vermes, *The Dead Sea Scrolls in English* (Penguin Books, Baltimore, 1962), used with permission.

15 Jesus, the Prophet

We had seen that the prophets from Moses, through Elijah, Elisha, and others sometimes performed miracles for the comfort of the people, for the confirmation of their faith, and for the glory of God. Jesus was probably fulfilling the role of Prophet rather than of Messiah when he performed his miracles for the people. But through these miracles he gives us a glimpse of someone greater than the Prophet. In this portion of his Gospel St. Matthew selects in an interesting fashion ten miracles to record.

MIRACLES OVER PHYSICAL DISEASES

Jesus, having been represented as the giver of the New Torah, came down from the Mount and was immediately confronted with a leper. Perhaps St. Matthew may have intended to show Jesus' attitude to the laws of uncleanness. In Matthew 8:1–4 the leper approached Jesus and ran the risk of ritually defiling him. According to the Mosaic law anyone who came into contact with leprosy, whether in a person, or in clothing, or in a house, became ritually polluted and was kept from the sanctuary and from fellowship with his coreligionists (Lev. 13–14). Jesus touched the leper, perhaps showing that he was willing to break the taboos for the purposes of charity. On the other hand, Jesus demonstrated his adherence to the law by requesting the leper to go to the priest according to the requirements which we find in Leviticus.

The Lord said to Moses, "This shall be the law of the leper for the day of his cleansing. He shall be brought to the priest; and the priest shall go out of the camp, and the priest shall make an examination. Then, if the leprous disease is healed in the leper, the priest shall command them to take for him who is to be cleansed two living clean birds and cedarwood and scarlet stuff and hyssop; and the priest shall command them to kill one of the birds in an earthen vessel over running water. He shall take the living bird with the cedarwood and the scarlet stuff and the hyssop, and dip them and the living bird in the blood of the bird that was killed over the running water; and he shall sprinkle it seven times upon him who is to be cleansed of leprosy; then he shall pronounce him clean, and shall let the living bird go into the open field. And he who is to be cleansed shall wash his clothes, and shave off all his hair, and bathe himself in water, and he shall be clean; and after that he shall come into the camp, but shall dwell outside his tent seven days. And on the seventh day he shall shave all his hair off his head; he shall shave off his beard and his eyebrows, all his hair. Then he shall wash his clothes, and bathe his body in water, and he shall be clean" (Lev. 14:1–9).

The second miracle, the healing of the centurion's servant, also appears to have a ritualistic aspect. The centurion was probably a Gentile or a convert to Judaism, and when he said that he was not worthy to have Christ enter into his house, he appeared to have been acknowledging the fact that his house and person were not sufficiently *kosher* for a Jewish teacher to associate with him. The centurion appeared to respect Jewish customs and advised Jesus just to give the commandment. Jesus in replying and commenting on the faith of the centurion said,

I tell you, many will come from the east and the west and sit at table with Abraham, Isaac, and Jacob in the kingdom of heaven, while the sons of the kingdom will be thrown into the outer darkness (Mt. 8:11–12).

With this statement Jesus transcended the kosher laws and foretold that the Gentiles would be accepted into the kingdom and would eat there the Messianic banquet with the patriarchs. To Jesus' audience this must have appeared to place him among the "avant garde" liberals.[1]

There is, perhaps, nothing spectacular about the curing of Peter's mother-in-law from her fever; it is another healing of physical disease.

All three miracles are physical cures, and St. Matthew sees them as the fulfillment of Isaiah 53:4 concerning the Suffering Servant.

Surely he has borne our griefs and carried our sorrows; yet we esteemed him stricken, smitten by God, and afflicted (Is. 53:4).

MIRACLES OVER PHYSICAL PHENOMENA, DEMONS, AND SIN

The next three miracles which St. Matthew elects to record reveal a little more of the character (person) of Jesus. In the first miracle Jesus stilled the storm at sea; he "rebuked the winds and the sea; and there was a great calm." The disciples then marveled and said,

---

[1] *Compare* the parable of Lazarus, Luke 16:19–31, where the characters experience a complete reversal of fortune. The rich man is excluded from the kingdom, but Lazarus, who is ritually unclean both on account of his sore and because he was licked by unclean animals, dogs, becomes the chief guest of honor, reclining in Abraham's bosom, that is, on the couch next to Abraham. Cf. John 13:25 where John is in a similar position to Jesus at the Last Supper.

What sort of man is this, that even winds and sea obey him? (Mt. 8:26–27).

They recognized in Jesus a power more than human, and yet we cannot say that they recognized him directly as the Son of God. In this account and in that of Mark 4:35–41 and Luke 8:22–25 the action evoked a question, but it did not supply an answer. This answer is partly indicated later in the Gospels, in Matthew 14:13–33, Mark 6:45–52, and John 6:16–21. In these passages it is recorded that Jesus walked upon the water; as he approached the frightened disciples, he proclaimed, "Take heart, it is I; have no fear." The conclusion of this episode found Peter trying to walk upon the sea to meet Jesus (Mt. 14:28–33), and when Jesus and Peter reached the boat,

. . . the wind ceased. And those in the boat worshiped him, saying, "Truly you are the Son of God" (Mt. 14:33).

Why did they recognize him then as the Son of God, whereas formerly they had only wondered what manner of man he was? The walking on the sea was intimately connected with the multiplication of the loaves which immediately preceded the walking on the water. Mark merely reports that when Jesus got into the boat, the men were "utterly astounded, for they did not understand about the loaves, but their hearts were hardened" (Mk. 6:51–52).

Why was the key to the apostles' understanding in the miracle of the loaves? Probably because the multiplication of the loaves was foreshadowed by the giving of the manna in the Old Testament (Ex. 16). According to some Jewish sources, when Yahweh gave the manna, he also effected what was known as a *gilluy Shekinah*, that is, an unbaring, an uncovering, of the Divine Presence, or, in other words, he manifested himself. Jesus revealed himself in the multiplication of the loaves, especially as seen in St. John's Gospel where this incident is connected with the giving of the manna in the Old Testament (Jn. 6). The people recognized Jesus as "the Prophet" (Deut. 18:15), but Jesus in the subsequent discourse revealed himself as more than this. He is the bread of life sent by the Father.

The Father or Yahweh gave manna in the wilderness, and in a similar way Jesus multiplied the loaves. But this was not all Yahweh did; he walked between the divided waters of the sea. These two events were associated in the Jewish mind and commemorated at the Passover in thanksgiving for the manifestation of Yahweh's presence, love, and power to Israel.[2] In this way the fourth miracle in St. Matthew's set of ten offers a glimpse of the divinity of Christ.

St. Matthew's next miracle shows Jesus' power over the supernatural powers of evil, the demons. In this strange miracle the demons recognized Jesus as the Son of God. They requested Jesus to cast them into a herd of swine. Jesus did so, and they perished in the waters. The account of this miracle is more detailed in Mark 5:1–20, and it is also given in Luke 8:26–39. Dr. Cave[3] has examined these pericopes[4] and has suggested that the additions in the narrative supplied by the other evangelists may have found their way into the Gospels from the synagogue readings for the time shortly after Passover.

These details, such as the breaking of chain and fetters (Mk. 5:4), remind one of Old Testament lessons, such as

[2] See Bertil Gartner, *John 6 and the Jewish Passover* (C. W. K. Gleerup, Lund, 1959), pp. 14–19.

[3] C. H. Cave, "The Obedience of Unclean Spirits," *New Testament Studies* 11 (1964), pp. 93–97.

[4] A pericope is a section of the scriptural text.

Judges 16 concerning Samson and the Philistines. But what is of more interest is the dialogue in Mark 5:7–12 wherein Jesus is addressed as the Son of the Most High God. "The Most High" (cf. Gen. 15:18; 2 Sam. 22:14; Ex. 15:1) was a title used in the Old Testament, usually by non-Israelites, to denote the God of Israel:[5] it is very appropriate in the Marcan text. Thus, Jesus was addressed by the demons in the same terms as Yahweh had been by idolaters. But there is, perhaps, also another reference to the Old Testament, namely, the herd falling into the sea; this may recall Exodus 14:27 ff.

The Lord routed the Egyptians in the midst of the sea. The waters returned and covered . . . all the host of Pharaoh . . . not so much as one of them remained.

These allusions to the Old Testament may not seem very convincing to us, but to the Hebrew to whom every syllable of scripture was pregnant with meaning these signs would be very important. Did Jesus here perform a prophetic *ôth*, with the swine representing the enemies of the true religion? It is possible that, in an action similar to the destruction of Pharaoh and his hosts by Yahweh, Jesus symbolized that he would destroy the powers of evil and rescue the chosen people.

Just as the Egyptians besought Moses to depart from Egypt (Ex. 12:31) after the plagues, so the people of this district begged Jesus to depart (Mt. 8:35). They must have been pagan people if they were rearing swine.

Thus, Jesus not only controls the physical elements like Yahweh but the demonic ones as well. He fulfilled the prophecy of Zechariah 13:2:

[5] Cave, *op. cit.*, p. 96.

I will remove from the land . . . the unclean spirit.

St. Matthew's sixth miracle (9:1–8) reveals a further aspect of Jesus' person. The miracle concerned the healing of the paralytic. However, it involved not only physical healing but also Jesus' pronouncement of the forgiveness of sin, which pronouncement evoked the criticism of the scribes, "This man is blaspheming," to which Mark and Luke add, "Who can forgive sins but God alone?" Jesus replied by proclaiming his authority on earth to forgive sin. Once again Jesus had done something which only Yahweh can do: only Yahweh can forgive sin.

THE LAST FOUR MIRACLES

The next miracles recorded by St. Matthew are the raising of Jairus' daughter and the healing of the woman with a hemorrhage. In these miracles Jesus broke through ritual taboos, for he permits the woman, who would defile him, according to Leviticus 15:19–32, to touch him, and he touches the dead girl, although contact with corpses also made one ritually unclean (Num. 19:11). In raising the girl from the dead Jesus had been foreshadowed by Elisha (2 Kings 4:32–37).

St. Matthew's list of miracles concludes with the healing of two blind men and a dumb demoniac. The blind men addressed Jesus as the Son of David. When the demoniac had been healed, the crowds marveled and said,

Never was anything like this seen in Israel (Mt.. 9:33).

But St. Matthew ends with the ominous remark,

But the Pharisees said, "He casts out demons by the prince of demons" (Mt. 9:34).

Ostensibly these miracles reveal Jesus primarily as the Prophet. They reflect to some extent the Elijah-Elisha motif, both in the performance of miracles and in that Elijah was expected to come to judge between the clean and the unclean. Jesus is represented, in not too obtrusive a way, as making decisions in these matters by his behavior. But apart from the ritualistic aspect the nature of the miracles fulfill Isaiah 35:5–6 and 61:1:

Then the eyes of the blind shall be opened, and the ears of the deaf unstopped; then shall the lame man leap like a hart, and the tongue of the dumb sing for joy. For waters shall break forth in the wilderness, and streams in the desert. . . .

The Spirit of the Lord God is upon me, because the Lord has anointed me to bring good tidings to the afflicted; he has sent me to bind up the broken-hearted, to proclaim liberty to the captives, and the opening of the prison to those who are bound. . . .

These two quotations summarize the point of the ten miracles enumerated by Matthew, as is evident by his recording of the question of John the Baptist and Jesus' response (Mt. 11:2–6). John asks, "Are you he who is to come, or shall we look for another?" The answer to John the Baptist recapitulates the character of Jesus as far as St. Matthew has shown it to us.

John may have expected Jesus to come in the figure of Elijah to bring judgment on the earth and to call to repentance; at this point he may have been seeking confirmation of this belief from Jesus. But what was important was Jesus' reply, for he answered according to the words of the prophet Isaiah, as quoted above.

However, it must be noted that, as far as one can see from the text of Isaiah, God himself is the agent of healing the blind, the deaf, and the dumb. In Isaiah 61:1 the agent is the Servant of Yahweh. It is probable that John the Baptist expected Jesus to behave with vengeance rather than with love, as did Elijah. But Jesus turned his attention to another direction, and to the people Jesus explained that John the Baptist is Elijah and that John has prepared the way for him who is to come.

By the nature of the miracles which he performed Jesus revealed himself as more than the Prophet, so that the people wondered what manner of man he was. He revealed himself as a man empowered to heal physical diseases and to modify ritual requirements; but more than this he appeared to play a role similar to Yahweh's. Thus, he controlled the natural phenomena; he walked through the waters and multiplied bread. Over and above this he claimed to forgive sin. St. Matthew's selection of miracles does not identify Jesus with Yahweh, but those miracles posed a difficult question of identification for the people of the time.

An ancient part of the Passover liturgy reads as follows:

Had he cleft the sea,
And not brought us through it   Jesus walks on the water
dryshod
It had sufficed us!

Had he brought us through it
dryshod,

And not sunk our oppressors in its depths It had sufficed us!	The Gadarene swine sink into the waters
Had he sunk our oppressors in its depths, And not satisfied our wants in the wilderness for forty years It had sufficed us!	Jesus multiplies the loaves
Had he satisfied our wants in the wilderness for forty years, And not fed us with manna It had sufficed us!	*" " "*

These words speak of the wonders and signs wrought by
Yahweh, and yet they are not wholly disconsonant with the
wonders and signs worked by Jesus, as is suggested in the
parallel columns above.

16 The Nature of the Kingdom

In the last chapter we saw the Prophet as one who appeared to be more than a man. The signs and wonders[1] which he performed had been foreshadowed in the first exodus or redemption[2] and had been prophesied for the second redemption by Second Isaiah.[3] The next section of St. Matthew which we choose to discuss is the parable-discourse in Chapter 13. In this section Jesus once again exhibited his gift of teaching and wisdom. Through the medium of parables he revealed the nature of the kingdom of heaven, which he was inaugurating. It is a kingdom unlike the kingdoms of the world which the devil offered Jesus during his temptation.

THE MEANING OF PARABLE

Parables were used frequently by Jewish teachers to illustrate their doctrine, and Jesus adopted the same method. A parable is usually described as a short story with one main

[1] Cf. Judah Goldin, trans., *The Fathers according to Rabbi Nathan* (Yale University Press, New Haven, 1955).

[2] There was a tradition that no handicapped person or unclean object was present on Mount Sinai during the first exodus.

[3] For the exodus motif in Second Isaiah see Bernard W. Anderson, "Exodus Typology in Second Isaiah," B. W. Anderson and Walter Harrelson, eds., *Israel's Prophetic Heritage* (Harper, New York, 1962), pp. 177–195.

175

point which the story illustrates: the details in the parable are not necessarily important and are usually taken from contemporary life. Most scholars would think that the parables as we have them in the New Testament are not exactly phrased as Jesus told them but were altered and expanded to be more consonant with the conditions and needs of the primitive Church communities in which they were told. Allegorical details are usually secondary or tertiary features in the parables. Arbitrary allegorization of parables, which finds meaning in every detail of the story—such as the early Church writers indulged in—is foreign both to Jesus' manner of teaching and also to the rabbinic teaching method. Thus, for example, it is not scholarly to find an allusion to the two sacraments of baptism and the Eucharist in the two pennies which the Good Samaritan gave to the innkeeper to pay for the patient's needs when he went away.

Nevertheless, there is one thing which we must remember. Although the Jewish teachers did not arbitrarily allegorize scripture or parables, they did have a way of interpreting scripture different from that of the modern scholar. Their interpretation was never divorced from the literal text of scripture, but they could make plays on words and deduct deeper meanings from texts by various methods. Let us take one example. They might take a word, for example, *benoth* (meaning daughters), remove the vowels (which were not printed in the text of their manuscripts), substitute other vowels—for instance, to make the word *bonoth* (meaning builders)—and then say that this text could refer to both builders and daughters. It seems very odd to us, but we must understand the New Testament and ancient Jewish writers according to their methodology, not according to ours. We shall see this particular point illustrated in the next chapter. But what we have pointed out is sufficient to show that the Jewish exegetical mind was very different from the modern mind in these matters.

Further, with regard to parables, many of the figures and symbols used in them can be traced back to Old Testament imagery. Modern schoalrs have suggested, therefore, that Jesus may have told his own parables after hearing the Hebrew scriptures read in the synagogue and thus may have used the words and symbols contained therein as the basis of his parables. If we could discover which scriptures were read on the occasions when Jesus taught, we should be able to understand more precisely his teaching. However, this is very difficult. As far as scholars can discover, the Old Testament was read in a three-year cycle: lessons were read from the Pentateuch (the first five books of the Old Testament), and then sections from the other books were read as a kind of extra reading. One can only experiment with various cycles and lectionaries and look up words and themes in the Old Testament, all of which does throw light on the parables. One thing can be said: parables are more than simple illustrative stories.

THE PARABLE OF THE SOWER

When we turn to St. Matthew's version of the parables of the kingdom, we find first of all the parable of the sower. In the Old Testament the chosen people frequently was spoken of in terms of seed, tree, and plants. God himself was said to plant and water them. For example, one can quote the well-known text of Isaiah 6:12–13 where the faithful remnant of Israel is spoken of as follows:

"... and the Lord removes men far away,
   and the forsaken places are many in the midst of the land.

And though a tenth remain in it,
  it will be burned again,
like a terebinth or an oak,
  whose stump remains standing when it is felled."
The holy seed is its stump (ital. mine).

Matthew quotes from this chapter of Isaiah after recording
the parable of the sower.

The establishment of the new covenant prophesied in
Jeremiah 31:27–34 is expressed in the same metaphor.

Behold, the days are coming, says the Lord, when I will sow the
house of Israel and the house of Judah with the seed of man
and the seed of beast. And it shall come to pass that as I have
watched over them to pluck up and break down, to overthrow,
destroy, and bring evil, so I will watch over them to build and to
plant, says the Lord. In those days they shall no longer say: "The
fathers have eaten sour grapes, and the children's teeth are set on
edge." But every one shall die for his own sin; each man who eats
sour grapes, his teeth shall be set on edge.

Behold, the days are coming, says the Lord, when I will make a
new covenant with the house of Israel and the house of Judah,
not like the covenant which I made with their fathers when I
took them by the hand to bring them out of the land of Egypt, my
covenant which they broke, though I was their husband, says the
Lord. But this is the covenant which I will make with the house
of Israel after those days, says the Lord: I will put my law
within them, and I will write it upon their hearts; and I will be
their God, and they shall be my people. And no longer shall each
man teach his neighbor and each his brother, saying, "Know the
Lord," for they shall all know me, from the least of them to the
greatest, says the Lord; for I will forgive their iniquity, and I
will remember their sin no more.[4]

---

[4] *Compare* St. John's sustained metaphor of the vine (Jn.15).

The descendant of David is described in an agricultural metaphor in Isaiah 11:1–3:

> There shall come forth a shoot from the stump of Jesse,
>   and a branch shall grow out of his roots.
> And the Spirit of the Lord shall rest upon him,
>   the spirit of wisdom and understanding,
>   the spirit of counsel and might,
>   the spirit of knowledge and the fear of the Lord.
> And his delight shall be in the fear of the Lord.

Therefore, when Jesus began to teach about a sower sowing seed, his Jewish audience would easily think either of the community of Israel, the planting of the Lord, or the word and teaching of God, which was often described as sowing seed; for example, Hillel said,

> When there are those who want to gather, you scatter [the
> seed of teaching]; when there are those who scatter, you gather.
> That is to say:
> If you see a generation to which the Torah is dear,
> you spread [its knowledge];
> but if you see a generation to which the Torah is not dear,
> you gather it and keep it to yourself.[5]

In fact, Jesus described the kingdom of heaven as the seed of men who were openly receptive to the Word of God; the Word of God is Jesus himself (*compare* Jas. 1:21 ff.).

Doctor C. H. Cave[6] in studying a possible lectionary back-

---

[5] Glatzer, *op. cit.*, p. 30. Jesus enunciates a similar principle when he explains why he speaks in parables (Mt. 13:13 ff.).

[6] C. H. Cave, "The Parables and the Scriptures," *New Testament Studies* 11 (July, 1965), pp. 374–387.

ground to the parable of the sower has suggested that the
parable recalls, among other texts, the following Old Testament passages:

For as the rain and the snow come down from heaven,
    and return not thither but water the earth,
making it bring forth and sprout,
    giving seed to the sower and bread to the eater . . . (Is. 55:10).

Blessed is the man who trusts in the Lord,
    whose trust is the Lord.
He is like a tree planted by water,
    that sends out its roots by the stream,
and does not fear when heat comes,
    for its leaves remain green,
and is not anxious in the year of drought,
    for it does not cease to bear fruit (Jer. 17:7–8).

For thus says the Lord to the men of Judah and to the inhabitants
        of Jerusalem:
    "Break up your fallow ground,
    and sow not among thorns" (Jer. 4:3).

Sow for yourselves righteousness,
    reap the fruit of steadfast love;
    break up your fallow ground,
for it is the time to seek the Lord,
    that he may come and rain salvation upon you (Hos. 10:12).

By examining the time of the liturgical year when these
would be read in the synagogue, Doctor Cave comes to
the conclusion that the "Parable of the Sower formed part of
an exhortation to repentance spoken on, or near to, the 9th
Ab [a fast day commemorating the fall of Jerusalem]. . . .

When the call to repentance fell on good ground, the results were fantastic."[7]

If Doctor Cave is correct, Jesus' parable at the fast commemorating the fall of Jerusalem teaches that the new community of the chosen people will be built upon repentance, the practice of righteousness and mercy, and acceptance of the Word of God, namely, Jesus himself. This is the kingdom, a community of the faithful, relying not on worldly advantages but solely on spiritual ones. The interpretation of the parable is consonant with the preaching of John the Baptist and appears to link the coming of the kingdom with the theology of the remnant of Israel.

THE PARABLE OF THE WEEDS

The second parable illustrates a further point about the kingdom. It is the parable of the enemy who sows weeds among the wheat. Doctor Cave has suggested that the parable may be part of a sermon for the Day of Atonement. Its purpose is to counsel patience. Among the Old Testament texts which it echoes may be Ezekiel 12:25 and 12:28:

But I the Lord will speak the word which I will speak, and it will be performed. It will no longer be delayed, but in your days, O rebellious house, I will speak the word and perform it, says the Lord God.

Therefore say to them, Thus says the Lord God: None of my words will be delayed any longer, but the word which I speak will be performed, says the Lord God.

Doctor Cave thinks that this may be a warning against

[7] Cave, *op. cit.*, p. 382.

forcing the issue of the kingdom by resorting, for example, to force of arms, such as the Jewish nationalists did from the second century B.C. into the first century A.D. Unlike the early Israelites, Jesus's kingdom is not established by exterminating alien powers but flourishes side by side with them. Jesus taught that the wicked should remain unmolested until the final judgment. Professor C. H. Dodd[8] compares this with the teaching of St. Paul in Corinthians 4:5.

Therefore do not pronounce judgment before the time, before the Lord comes, who will bring to light the things now hidden in darkness and will disclose the purpose of the heart. Then every man will receive his commendation from God.

The parable, as Professor J. Jeremias[9] stresses, is eschatological in character, that is, it looks toward the end of time.

THE MUSTARD SEED

St. Matthew's third parable is that of the mustard seed. Doctor Cave has suggested as its background Ezekiel 17:22–24:

Thus says the Lord God: "I myself will take a sprig from the lofty top of the cedar, and will set it out; I will break off from the topmost of its young twigs a tender one, and I myself will plant it upon a high and lofty mountain; on the mountain height of Israel will I plant it, that it may bring forth boughs and bear fruit, and become a noble cedar; and under it will dwell all kinds of beasts; in the shade of its branches birds of every sort will nest. And all the trees of the field shall know that I the Lord bring low

8 C. H. Dodd, *The Parables of the Kingdom*, rev. ed. (Scribner, New York, 1961), pp. 147 ff.

9 J. Jeremias, *The Parables of Jesus*, trans. by S. H. Hooke, 6th ed. (Scribner, New York, 1963), pp. 224–227.

the high tree, and make high the low tree, dry up the green tree, and make the dry tree flourish. I the Lord have spoken, and I will do it."

The Jews contemporary with Jesus interpreted this passage as a reference to a mighty king who would arise[10] and with whom would dwell the righteous and the humble. There is also a later Jewish work in which the simile of mustard seed is used in an illustration referring to the Gentile converts who will find shelter in Israel.[11] If this interpretation is correct, then the mustard seed probably adds a further point to the preceding parable: not only are the aliens' powers not destroyed, but "foreigners" will receive protection from the ruler of the kingdom.[12] Professor Dodd[13] avers that the main point of the parable is not the smallness of the seed but its growth as a tree to the point where it can shelter the birds. In one Jewish commentary "the birds of heaven" signify the Gentiles. Thus, the kingdom is not only for the Jewish people; this is especially obvious by Christ's use of the word "shelter," which in the Greek is "actually an eschatological technical term for the incorporation of the Gentiles into the people of God . . ."[14]

The three parables reveal step by step the character of the kingdom. First, God sends his Word to be received by the chosen people, but then he allows the faithful and the faithless to grow side by side until the final judgment. Finally, the mustard seed parable looks toward the inclusion of the Gentiles in the kingdom.[15] Matthew 13 concludes with the

[10] *Compare* Ezekiel 31 and Daniel 4.
[11] Cave, *op. cit.*, p. 386.
[12] *Compare* Isaiah 56.
[13] Dodd, *op. cit.*, p. 153.
[14] Jeremias, *op. cit.*, p. 147.
[15] The parable of the leaven forms a pair with that of the mustard seed. See Jeremias, *op. cit.*, pp. 147 ff.; Dodd, *op. cit.*, pp. 154 ff.

three short parables concerning the treasure, the pearl, and the drop net. The kingdom has arrived and the harvest is approaching, but those who will be saved must be prepared to place the king and the kingdom above everything else. The members-elect of the kingdom must have the perspicacity and faith to accept the person of Christ, the Word. Matthew 16 shows this discernment and faith and the subsequent proclamation of the building of the kingdom.

THE PROCLAMATION OF THE PLANTING OF THE KINGDOM

In Chapter 16 St. Matthew records Jesus' coming to Caesarea Philippi. Some would place this incident after the Resurrection, but in any case, perhaps it is well to see it in its place within Matthew's theology of the kingdom, for his Gospel especially emphasizes the Church as community.

Jesus asked his disciples about the conclusions at which people had arrived concerning his identity—indeed, what manner of man he was. The question presupposed a certain lively discussion on the point. The candidates finally presented were John the Baptist, Elijah, Jeremiah, or one of the prophets. Jesus then asked for a decision on the part of his disciples. All three synoptic Gospels record that Peter replied, "You are the Christ," to which phrase St. Matthew adds, "the Son of the living God." This addition placed Jesus in a role other than that of merely the Prophet or the Messiah, the one anointed or designated by God, and in an entirely different dimension. St. Matthew must have meant his readers to understand "Son of God" in a sense different from that in which we speak of Christians as the sons and daughters of God. Indeed, Peter used the definite article— *the* Son of the Living God—and Jesus commented that he could not have attained this insight by human intelligence but only through a special revelation from the Father.

Blessed are you, Simon Bar-Jona! For flesh and blood has not revealed this to you, but my Father who is in heaven (Mt. 16:17).

It would seem that Peter realized—if only for a fleeting moment—the divinity of Christ, even though many scholars would deny this. This realization was to be confirmed in the post-Easter faith of the early Church. As Jesus himself prophesied in John 14:26,

. . . the Counselor, the Holy Spirit, whom the Father will send in my name, he will teach you all things, and bring to your remembrance all that I have said to you.

The declaration of the divinity of Christ was the raison d'être of the Christian community in the same way as the confession of monotheism was the raison d'être of the community of the descendants of Abraham.[16] Hence, it is understandable that Peter's confession was followed by Jesus' declaration of the establishment of the New Assembly. Indeed, it is possible to see the commission to Peter as the full realization of the promises and covenant between God and Abraham, with Peter as the fulfillment of the type of Abraham. One might suggest the following parallels:[17]

Abraham	*Peter*
Abraham was supposed to be the first human being to acknowledge the true nature of God and to recognize him as supreme God of heaven and earth.	Peter was the first to recognize the true nature of Jesus and acknowledge him as Christ and the Son of God.

[16] *Compare,* for example, the First Epistle of St. John.

[17] This is elaborated in more detail in my article " 'Thou art' Abraham 'and upon this Rock,' " *Heythrop Journal* (July, 1965), pp. 289–301.

This revelation was supposed to have come to Abraham directly from God. He did not acquire it from human teaching.	Peter does not realize this by human intelligence but through a revelation from God the Father.
In biblical and extra-biblical writing Abraham is called a "rock."	Peter is called *Petros,* stone or rock.
God builds up a new elect community through Abraham, i.e., Abraham is a physical progenitor.	God founds the new community on Peter, that is, he is a spiritual progenitor.
God promised immunity and perpetuity to the seed of Abraham: they would escape the fire of Gehenna (hell).	God promised that the gates of Hades should never prevail against the Church.

Therefore, Peter may be the fulfillment of the type of Abraham; he may be the new Abraham of the new covenant. This is consonant with St. Matthew's theology, for he begins his Gospel with the genealogy of Christ from Abraham and ends with the world-wide mission of Christ's Church.

Furthermore, the Church thus founded is not to be envisaged in architectural images or in legalistic terms but as a temple consisting of living men and women, a chosen family or race. This family or race is not a static, unchanging entity but a vital and growing community, which has inherited both the promises and responsibilities of Abraham and Sarah. Moreover, this community like the suffering community of Israel and the Suffering Servant Jesus was destined to undergo travail and torment. As Jesus said in John 16:20–22,

Truly, truly, I say to you, you will weep and lament, but the world will rejoice; you will be sorrowful, but your sorrow will turn into joy. When a woman is in travail she has sorrow, because her hour has come; but when she is delivered of the child, she no longer remembers the anguish, for joy that a child is born into the world. So you have sorrow now, but I will see you again and your hearts will rejoice, and no one will take your joy from you.

However, the suffering of the community is precisely a productive suffering like childbirth. It brings new life and new members into the sphere of salvation. Such a productive suffering was anticipated in Judaism. A noble expression of this is found in one of the thanksgiving psalms discovered among the Dead Sea Scrolls.

> Yea, I am in distress
> as a woman in travail
> bringing forth her firstborn,
> when, as her time draws near,
> the pangs come swiftly upon her
> and all the grievous throes
> that rack those heavy with child.
>
> For now, amid throes of death,
> new life is coming to birth,
> and the pangs of travail set in,
> as at last there enters the world
> the man-child long conceived.
> Now, amid throes of death,
> that man-child long foretold
> is about to be brought forth.
> Now, amid pangs of hell,
> there will burst forth from the womb
> that marvel of mind and might,
> and that man-child will spring from the throes!
> Delivery comes apace

for him that now lies in the womb;
as the hour of his birth draws near,
the pangs begin!
   Come too the grievous throes,
the racking birth-pains come
upon all that bear in the womb
the seeds of the new life!

   Yet, likewise unto them
that carry in their womb
the seeds of worthless things
are come the grievous throes,
the pangs of hell and the torment.
   For lo, the wall shall rock
unto its prime foundation,
even as rocks a ship
stormtossed on the waters.

   The heavens shall thunder loud,
and they that now do dwell
on the crumbling dust of the earth
be as sailors on the seas,
aghast at the roaring of the waters;
and all the wise men thereof
be as mariners on the deep
when all their skill is confounded
by the roaring of the seas,
the seething of the depths,
the swirling of the tides.

   High shall the billows [surge,]
loud the breakers roar;
and, even as they surge,
the gates of Hell shall be opened,
Perditions's shafts be loosed.
   Down shall they go screaming to the abyss,

and the gates of [Hell] shall open
upon all worthless things,
and the doors of Perdition shall close
on all the iniquity
which they would yet bring forth;
and the bars of eternity
on all unworthy intent.

I give thanks unto Thee, O Lord,
for Thou hast freed my soul from the pit.
and drawn me up from the slough of hell
to the crest of the world.
So walk I on uplands unbounded
and know that there is hope
for that which Thou didst mold out of dust
to have consort with things eternal.
For lo, Thou hast taken a spirit
distorted by sin,
and purged it of the taint of much transgression,
and given it a place
in the host of the holy beings,
and brought it into communion
with the sons of heaven.
Thou hast made a mere man to share
the lot of the Spirits of Knowledge,
to praise Thy name in their chorus
and rehearse Thy wondrous deeds
before all Thy works.

I, that am molded of clay,
what am I?
I, that am kneaded with water,
what is my worth?
I, that have taken my stand
where wickedness reigns,
that have cast my lot with the froward;

whose soul has lodged like a beggar
in a place of wild unrest;
I, whose every step
has been amid ruin and rout—
on what strength of mine own may I count. . . .[18]

FURTHER READING

Dodd, C. H., *The Parables of the Kingdom,* rev. ed. Scribner, New York, 1961.

Fuller, R. H., *Interpreting the Miracles.* Westminster, Philadelphia, 1963.

Jeremias, J., *The Parables of Jesus,* trans. by S. H. Hooke. Scribner, New York, 1963.

Lewis, C. S., *Miracles.* Macmillan, New York, 1947 (paperback).

[18] Gaster, *op. cit.,* 143–145.

17 The Passion of God

WHY WAS JESUS EXPECTED TO SUFFER?

Jesus in his role as the Prophet might have been expected to suffer on behalf of the community. Suffering by the Servant of Yahweh, who is probably a prophet, had been foretold, as we have seen, in the Servant Songs of Second Isaiah. Yahweh himself is compared to a woman in labor, for example, in Isaiah 42:14:

> For a long time I have held my peace,
> I have kept still and restrained myself;
> now I will cry out like a woman in travail,
> I will gasp and pant.

And the Servant himself was to suffer as an atoning sacrifice for the people, but he would see the efficacy of his trials, for example, Isaiah 53:10–11:

Yet it was the will of the Lord to bruise him;
  he has put him to grief;
when he makes himself an offering for sin,
  he shall see his offspring, he shall prolong his days;
the will of the Lord shall prosper in his hand;
  he shall see the fruit of the travail of his soul and be satisfied;
by his knowledge shall the righteous one, my servant,
  make many to be accounted righteous;
and he shall bear their iniquities.

191

Why, then, did Peter refuse to believe that Jesus was destined to suffer? He exclaimed after Jesus' first prediction of his passion,

God forbid, Lord! This shall never happen to you (Mt. 16:22).

Because Peter accepted Jesus as the Messiah, he would not expect him to suffer since there was practically no tradition in Judaism concerning a suffering Messiah. Peter, remembering Hillel, who was nearly lynched, or Zechariah, who was murdered between the sanctuary and the altar (Mt. 23:35), might have seen some danger for Jesus, but he probably thought that Jesus in his capacity of Messiah and as the Son of God would overcome this.

Why then did Jesus expect the disciples to understand that it was necessary for him to suffer? Perhaps because if they had understood the scriptures, they might have seen "the definite plan and foreknowledge of God" whereby Jesus, the Son of God, was indeed destined to suffer.

GENESIS 15, THE COVENANT OF THE PIECES

We have observed in Chapter 1 that at the covenant of the pieces Yahweh himself walked through the symbols of death, taking the curse of the broken covenant upon himself.

If the Petrine confession recalls the promises to Abraham, then, perhaps, the predictions of the Passion, which in all three synoptic Gospels occur directly after the Petrine confession, are also meant to be understood against the background of Genesis 15, namely, the death of Yahweh. It is to be noted that the bible only records that Yahweh walked through the lane of slaughtered animals: Abraham was in a deep trance. One is able to confirm that perhaps the passion

of Jesus may be understood from Genesis 15 if one turns to
the extra-biblical traditions about the covenant of the pieces.

Abraham is reputed to have received a series of visions
from God on that night of the covenant of the pieces. He
saw this world and the world to come; the history of Israel
and the kingdoms which would subdue her; the end of the
reign of evil by the Messiah and/or *the person whom God
would take and use to make atonement for all Israel.* In one
text it is hinted that this person will be more than a man.
The atonement wrought by this person, who will be of the
seed of Abraham, will supersede all atoning sacrifices and
all Temple services and will also draw the Gentiles into the
chosen people.[1]

It is this vision of him who is to come, experienced by
Abraham, to which Jesus may have referred when he said in
John 8:56–59 ff.,

"Your father Abraham rejoiced to see my day; he saw it and was
glad." The Jews then said to him, "You are not yet fifty years old,
and have you seen Abraham?" [Some manuscripts read, "has
Abraham seen you?"] Jesus said to them, "Truly, truly, I say to
you, before Abraham was, I am." So they took up stones to throw
at him . . .

In the same chapter (Jn. 8:40) Jesus had spoken of the
attempt upon his life. Thus, in this chapter Jesus spoke of
his expected death and made a claim to preexistence and
oneness with God, the latter by using the "I am," that is,
the divine name given at the revelation of the burning
bush in Exodus 3:14.

[1] See especially *The Apocalypse of Abraham*, trans. by G. H. Box
(S.P.C.K., London, 1918). The date of this work is uncertain but similar
traditions are found in *Jubilees*, which is an extra-biblical but pre-Christian
work.

GENESIS 22, THE BINDING OF ISAAC

But Genesis 15 is not the only scripture which may implicitly prophesy the death of the God-man. We have spoken in Chapter 3 about the tradition concerning the Binding of Isaac in Genesis 22. In this text Abraham appeared to think that God wished the sacrificial death of his son, Isaac. God refused this sacrifice and promised that he would provide on Mount Moriah. Further, he renewed his promises to Abraham and confirmed these by swearing by himself (literally "by his own life").

We have seen also that the extra-biblical traditions about Isaac saw his sacrifice as one which wrought atonement for sin and for the benefit and sanctification of mankind. Isaac was the prototype of the martyr and the prototype of the resurrected man. However, Isaac did not really die on Mount Moriah and he was not resurrected. Nevertheless, this doctrine prepared the Jews for one who might be destined to fulfill these earnest expectations. Certainly, St. Paul used the theology of the Binding of Isaac to explain the redemptive work of Christ—his atoning death and resurrection. Some scholars link the traditions concerning Isaac to the figure of the Suffering Servant of Isaiah.[2]

THE PERSECUTION OF THE PROPHETS

However, the Suffering Servant is typical of the great line of prophets from Micaiah, Elijah, Amos, Jeremiah,[3] and on through Ezra[4] and his spiritual descendants, the School of

[2] See the bibliography listed after Chapter 3.
[3] There is much affinity between Jesus and Jeremiah.
[4] The association between Ezra and Hillel is suggested in the following dictum: "In ancient days when the Torah was forgotten from Israel, Ezra

Hillel, all of whom suffered for the sake of God's covenant. Perhaps we may say that whereas the cause of Jesus' passion certainly seemed to be his claim to divinity, the indirect cause lay in the continual opposition of the recalcitrant materialistically-minded sons of Abraham to those who witnessed against their infidelity to the covenant love of Yahweh.

Thus, as Jesus entered on the final stage of his earthly life, St. Matthew portrays him as the Prophet. However, before Matthew does so, he throws into relief the political Messiahship, which could have been Christ's, had he wished it.

SIC TRANSIT GLORIA MUNDI

Jesus approached Jerusalem probably to attend a feast, possibly Hanukkah[5] or Passover. He requested the disciples to procure an ass tied with her colt. St. Mark says that this was at the crossroad, but the text may read that the animal was tied "to a vine." In this case Jesus fulfilled the prophecy of Genesis 49:10–11 concerning the descendant from the tribe of Judah.

The sceptre shall not depart from Judah,
    nor the ruler's staff from between his feet,
until he comes to whom it belongs;
    and to him shall be the obedience of the peoples.
Binding his foal to the vine
    and his ass's colt to the choice vine,
he washes his garments in wine
    and his vesture in the blood of grapes . . . (ital. mine).

---

came up from Babylon and reestablished it. Then it was again forgotten until Hillel the Babylonian came up and reestablished it" *Sukkah* 20a. The prophetic movement and the Pharisees seemed to be linked.

[5] The feast of the Dedication of the Temple (cf. 1 Macc. 13:51).

It has been conjectured also that Jesus may have made use of the occasion of an agricultural festival coinciding with the feast at which a man was chosen to be king and to ride on an ass among the people. It may be that this was so. On whatever occasion this procession took place, St. Matthew saw the incident as the fulfillment of Isaiah 62:11 and of Zechariah 9:9.

> Behold, the Lord has proclaimed
>   to the end of the earth:
> Say to the daughter of Zion,
>   "Behold, your salvation comes;
>   behold, his reward is with him,
>   and his recompense before him."
>
> Rejoice greatly, O daughter of Zion!
>   Shout aloud, O daughter of Jerusalem!
> Lo, your king comes to you;
>   triumphant and victorious is he,
>   humble and riding on an ass,
>   on a colt the foal of an ass.

The whole city was stirred. Perhaps the people entertained the hope of political victory and freedom, of an autonomous Jewish State. For Jesus appeared to act in deliberate fulfillment of Zechariah 9:9, laying claim to the homage of the people. He acted openly, indeed provocatively. The crowd threw down their garments just as the early Israelites did in 2 Kings 9 at the proclamation of Jehu as king:

Then in haste every man of them took his garment, and put it under him on the bare steps, and they blew the trumpet, and proclaimed, "Jehu is king" (2 Kings 9:13).

In Jesus' case the crowds cried out, "Hosanna" ("save now" or a cry of joy, which comes from Psalm 118:26 ff.) and "Blessed is he who comes" (in its original usage this was a blessing invoked upon the pilgrim who approached the Holy City for a festival). They hailed Jesus as a king, and it may well have been the disappointment of this political hope which turned Judas Iscariot and others against him.[6]

Jesus entered the city and cleansed the Temple, driving out the merchants. His statement approximated Jeremiah 7:11:

Has this house, which is called by my name, become a den of robbers in your eyes? Behold, I myself have seen it, says the Lord.

It is related also to Isaiah 56:7–8:

... these [foreigners] I will bring to my holy mountain,
    and make them joyful in my house of prayer;
their burnt offerings and their sacrifices
    will be accepted on my altar;
for my house shall be called a house of prayer
    for all peoples.
Thus says the Lord God,
    who gathers the outcasts of Israel,
I will gather yet others to him
    besides those already gathered.

JESUS' FINAL PROPHECIES

Jesus returned to Bethany and lodged there (Mt. 21:14). In the morning he cursed the fig tree, and it withered (Mt.

---

[6] The prophets were certainly involved in politics. In 2 Kings it was Elisha who ordered the anointing of Jehu.

21:18–22). Probably this may be regarded as another prophetic ôth, the fig tree symbolizing either Israel, which bore no fruit, or the Jewish teachers, who met under fig trees for their studies.[7] If so, it is a fitting prelude to the controversy over Jesus' teaching authority. After this action Jesus entered the temple, and the chief priests and elders of the people began to question his authority to do these things. Jesus replied by asking them what they thought about the authority of John the Baptist. The chief priests and elders were afraid to deny the authority of John because of the people. They refused to answer Jesus' question, and therefore Jesus did not answer theirs. However, St. Matthew reports that Jesus told another group of parables which were designed to challenge the hearers to make a decision concerning Jesus' mission and to come to a resolution of the problem of his authority. The parables, scattered through Matthew 21 to 25, are some of the richest and most dramatic in the Gospels.

1. *The parable of the two sons.* In this parable (Mt. 21:28–32) Jesus showed that those who repent would be saved before the "pious." The parable may have been directed against the hypocritical Pharisees—would they receive the message of the kingdom?[8]

2. *The parable of the householder with the vineyard.* The background to this parable (Mt. 21:33–43) is the Song of the Vineyard, which is found in Isaiah 5:1–7:

> Let me sing for my beloved
> a love song concerning his vineyard:

---

[7] *Compare* John 2:48.

[8] It has been suggested that the story of Esau and Jacob is behind this parable. If so, Esau is preferred to Jacob.

My beloved had a vineyard
   on a very fertile hill.
He digged it and cleared it of stones,
   and planted it with choice vines;
he built a watchtower in the midst of it,
   and hewed out a wine vat in it;
and he looked for it to yield grapes,
   but it yielded wild grapes.
And now, O inhabitants of Jerusalem
   and men of Judah,
judge, I pray you, between me
   and my vineyard.
What more was there to do for my vineyard,
   that I have not done in it?
When I looked for it to yield grapes,
   why did it yield wild grapes?
And now I will tell you
   what I will do to my vineyard.
I will remove its hedge,
   and it shall be devoured;
I will break down its wall,
   and it shall be trampled down.
I will make it a waste;
   it shall not be pruned or hoed,
   and briers and thorns shall grow up;
I will also command the clouds
   that they rain no rain upon it.
For the vineyard of the Lord of hosts
   is the house of Israel,
and the men of Judah
   are his pleasant planting;
and he looked for justice,
   but behold, bloodshed;
for righteousness,
   but behold, a cry!

The parable illustrated Israel's rejection of the prophets and then of Jesus himself. To the parable the early Church community added the text from Psalm 118:22–23 concerning the stone which the builders rejected. Here there may be the familiar play on the words "son" and "stone," "builders" and "daughters," i.e., the Sanhedrin. In this parable Jesus warned the Jewish leaders that the kingdom would be removed from them and given to others. The chief priests and Pharisees realized that he was speaking about them (Mt. 22:45), but they feared the crowds and so made no real attempt to arrest him.

3. *The parable of the wedding feast.* According to Matthew 22:1–14 Jesus enforced his point with a further parable to which St. Matthew has added an appendix about the wedding garment. The parable in St. Matthew's version tells of the marriage feast which a king made for his son. The guests who were invited made excuses and the people from the thoroughfares were then invited. The parable reflects the lightheartedness of the materialistic Sadducees who owned many large farms and estates in the Galilean hills: they had no interest in the messianic banquet. But also, as we saw in Chapter 11, the wedding feast reflected the espousal of God and Israel in the covenant: the Sadducees behaved in a similar way to the worshipers of Baal in Hosea.

The struggle between the teaching of Jesus and that of the Pharisees and the Sadducees continues in Matthew 22:15–45 until it reaches the point of the forced but silent submission that Jesus is Lord (Mt. 22:46).

According to Matthew 23 Jesus delivered his woes against the Pharisees in the same manner as the early prophets had delivered their woes against the people. But as Asher Finkel has shown, these appear to be directed exclusively to the School of Shammai. Following these woes is Jesus' lament over Jerusalem, concluding with his statement that her house will be desolate and forsaken.[9] In Matthew 24 Jesus foretold the manifold sufferings to come at the end of time.[10] Matthew 25:1–13 tells the parable of the ten virgins, probably a story with its background in both Exodus 19 and 24, which describe the giving of the law on Mount Sinai. Its main indication seems to be that the Jewish teachers will be excluded from the kingdom because they have not accompanied their teaching with good works.

This parable is followed by that of the talents (Mt. 25:14–30), which is probably directed once again toward the teachers who may have kept their privileges to themselves instead of sharing them.

The parables[11] end with the picture of the Son of Man coming in his glory to assist at the judgment seat (Mt. 25:31–46). The background to this section is probably Ezekiel 34. In that passage God rebukes the leaders (kings and rulers) of Israel for abusing their power and says that he himself will accept the responsibilities which they have failed to implement and that he will care for the people. In Ezekiel 34 the good kings are divided from the bad.

C. F. Burney has translated this section into Hebrew poetry and has suggested that this may be the original language of the section. The following is a translation of the poem.[12]

---

[9] One might compare this to the dirge which Amos sings over the Virgin Israel (Amos 5). The desolation probably means the departure of the Shekinah.

[10] *Compare* Amos' theology of the Day of the Lord, pp. 93 f. above.

[11] The author has discussed these parables in a little more detail in "The Parable of the Foolish Scholars," *Novum Testamentum* 9, Fasc. 2 (1967), pp. 107–123.

[12] C. F. Burney, "Matthew xxv, 31–46, as a Hebrew Poem," *Journal of Theological Studies* 14 (1913), pp. 414–424, by permission of the Clarendon Press, Oxford.

When the Son of man shall come in His glory,
And all the angels with Him.
He shall sit on the throne of His glory.
And all nations shall be gathered before Him,
And He shall separate them one from another,
As the shepherd doth separate the sheep
   from among the goats;
And He shall set the sheep on His right hand,
   But the goats on His left hand.

Then the king shall say to those on His right hand,
   Come, ye blessed of My Father,
Inherit the kingdom prepared for you
   From the foundation of the world.
For hungry was I, and ye fed me;
Thirsty was I, and ye relieved me;
A stranger was I, and ye housed me;
   Naked, and ye clothed me;
Sick was I, and ye visited me;
In prison was I, and ye came to me.
Then shall the righteous make answer to Him, saying,
Lord,
When saw we Thee hungry, and sustained Thee,
   Or thirsty, and relieved Thee?
When saw we Thee a stranger, and housed Thee,
   Or naked, and clothed Thee?
When saw we Thee sick, and visited Thee,
   Or in prison, and came to Thee?

Then the king shall answer and say unto them,
   That which ye did unto one of these least of My brethren,
   To Me too ye did it.
Then He shall say to those also on His left hand,
Depart from Me, ye accursed,
   Into fire everlasting,

Prepared for the Devil and his angels.
For hungry was I, and ye fed Me not;
Thirsty was I, and ye relieved Me not;
A stranger was I, and ye housed Me not;
   Naked, and ye clothed Me not;
Sick and in prison, and ye visited Me not.
Then they too shall make answer, saying,
Lord,
When saw we Thee either hungry or thirsty
Or stranger or naked or sick or in prison,
   And did not minister to Thee?

And He shall make answer to them, saying,
That which ye did not to one of these least of My breathren,
   To Me too ye did it not.

And these shall depart to chastisement everlasting,
But the righteous to life everlasting.

The cleansing of the Temple augured a new liturgical era for Israel. The cursing of the fig tree condemned useless academic disputes which bore no fruit and could not satisfy the Son of Man. The parable of the two sons suggested that those who had been called first by Yahweh would be rejected. The parable of the tenants of the vineyard prophesied the termination of the contemporary ruling power in Israel. The parable of the wedding feast reflected the exclusion of the chief guests from the covenant celebration of God and Israel.

The woes against the Shammaites cast a type of ominous potent "curse" upon those who had broken the covenant of Yahweh,[13] and Jesus' lament over Jerusalem presaged the

---

[13] *Compare* the curses in Deuteronomy 27:15-26.

passing away of the old order, the passing away of the Shekinah (the presence of God) from Jerusalem. The parable of the ten virgins excluded the teachers, who had no good works to accompany their teaching, from the bridal chamber of Yahweh, from the nuptial covenant sealed by the descent of the Shekinah. The picture of the day of Judgment recalled the theme of the Day of the Lord frequently mentioned by the prophets and dramatized the rejection of the leaders of Israel and the salvation of those Jews and Gentiles who had practiced deeds of loving kindness.

Thus, the scriptures—Genesis 15, Genesis 22, and Second Isaiah—together with the sufferings and warnings of the prophets of God should have led the disciples to understand that Moses and all the prophets, the defenders of the covenant, had foretold that Christ should suffer and enter into his glory (*compare* Lk. 24:25 ff.). The time for Yahweh to take the curse upon himself had arrived.

When Jesus had finished these sayings, he turned his disciples' thoughts to the Passover, when the Son of Man, the Second Isaac, the Lamb of God, would be crucified (Mt. 26:1–2).

FURTHER READING

Blinzler, Josef, *The Trial of Jesus,* trans. by Isabel and Florence McHugh. Newman, Westminster, Maryland, 1959.

Finkel, Ashur, *The Pharisees and the Teacher of Nazareth.* Leiden, 1964, pp. 136 ff.

Taylor, Vincent, *Jesus and His Sacrifice.* St. Martin's Press, New York, 1959.

18 The Supreme Covenant Meal

Living out each detail of salvation history, Jesus approached the night before he was betrayed. The expected redemption was to occur at the Passover.[1] By the time of Jesus the following events were commemorated on that night:

1. Creation
2. The Covenant of the Pieces
3. The Binding of Isaac
4. The Passover
5. The Bringing Forth from Egypt
6. The Future Redemption

These events were supposed to have happened on the same day in the year, the fifteenth of Nisan.[2]

It was no wonder that Jesus chose the feast of Passover during which to implement the climax of salvation history. Yet, if Jesus, like Isaac and the lamb, was to be the sacrificial victim, we must ask whether it would not have been appropriate for him to die on the feast day itself. Apparently, according to the synoptic Gospels, he died on the day after he had celebrated the Passover.

Although St. John's Gospel does not record the institution

---

[1] See pp. 53 ff. above.

[2] Naturally, there is no means whereby to discover the date, but the interesting point lies in the fact that they were theologically associated.

of the Eucharist, it does speak as though Jesus was crucified at the time when the lambs for the Passover were being slain in the Temple in preparation for the Passover meal that evening. That is, they would have been slain on Friday afternoon for the feast which began on Friday evening and continued into Saturday (*compare* Jn. 13:1; 18:28; 19:14).

St. John also seems to depict Jesus as the Paschal Lamb by noting three Passover details which were related to Jesus' death. First, he mentions the hyssop[3] (Jn. 19:29). Second, he stresses the fact that Jesus' legs were not broken; this was in fulfillment of Exodus 12:46 which required that the paschal victim's bones should not be broken. Third, John and some manuscripts of Matthew mention the piercing of Jesus' side. The "kosher" killing of a victim required that it should be pierced with a movable object and that uncongealed blood should spurt out.[4]

John, by bearing witness to these three details, appears to stress their importance (Jn. 19:36):

For these things took place that the scripture might be fulfilled, "Not a bone of him shall be broken."

Thus, for John, Jesus appears to be the Lamb of God, which, by its association with Isaac and the sacrifices of the Temple, was thought to take away the sin of the world. And for John, that Lamb died as the lambs for the feast were being slaughtered in the Temple. Jesus joined his own sacrifice to the sacrifices of the former order and by so doing elevated them and also superseded them. As the author of the Epistle to the Hebrews writes in Hebrews 10:5–10,

---

[3] This action is mentioned by the other evangelists, too.

[4] For further details see the author's "Mingled Blood from the Side of Christ," *New Testament Studies*, forthcoming.

"Sacrifices and offerings thou hast not desired, but a body hast thou prepared for me; in burnt offerings and sin offerings thou hast taken no pleasure. Then I said, 'Lo, I have come to do thy will, O God,' as it is written of me in the roll of the book." When he said above, "Thou hast neither desired nor taken pleasure in sacrifices and offerings and burnt offerings and sin offerings" (these are offered according to the law), then he added, "Lo, I have come to do thy will." He abolishes the first in order to establish the second. And by that will we have been sanctified through the offering of the body of Jesus Christ once for all.

THE APPARENT INCONSISTENCY BETWEEN JOHN AND THE SYNOPTICS

There is, however, a difficulty. If Jesus died before the eating of the Passover meal, then the Eucharist must have been instituted at an ordinary meal, not the Passover. This might seriously affect the whole theology of the Eucharist, which would lose the elements of a covenant and sacrificial meal. It would be, perhaps, little more than a mere party held by Jesus with his friends before his death. It is difficult to imagine Jesus eating the paschal meal early for his convenience, but it is also difficult not to find inconsistencies between John and the synoptic Gospels in their dating of Jesus' death and their description of the character of the Last Supper.

A RESOLUTION OF THESE DIFFICULTIES

A resolution of these difficulties has been discovered and the chief exponent of this is Annie Jaubert.[5] Evidence has been discovered which shows that two liturgical calendars

[5] Annie Jaubert, *The Date of the Last Supper*, trans. by Isaac Rafferty (Alba, New York, 1965).

were in use among the Jews contemporary with Christ. One was a solar calendar according to which the feasts fell on the same day of the week each year. Thus, the Passover would always fall on Wednesday, though the feast would begin the evening before. It appears that this calendar was used by the Qumran community and probably by other Jews. The Jerusalem priesthood appeared to use the lunar calendar; according to this calendar the feasts fell on different days of the week each year.

It is thought that it was possible that Jesus and his friends celebrated the Passover according to the solar calendar on Tuesday evening. Thus, the crucifixion would have taken place on Friday while the "lunar lambs" were being slain in the Temple. If this theory is correct, and it has won quite widespread approval, then Jesus both kept the Passover and instituted the Eucharist on that occasion but also was crucified on the Passover.

This chronology is not disproved by early Christian writings. One early work, the *Didascalia*, reads as follows:

After eating the Pasch, on *Tuesday evening*, we went to the Mt. of Olives and, in the night, they took our Lord Jesus. The following day, which is *Wednesday*, he was kept in the house of the high priest, Caiphas; the same day the leaders of the people met and discussed his case. The following day, *Thursday*, they brought him to the governor, Pilate, and he was kept with Pilate through the night following Thursday. On the morning of the *Friday* they made many accusations concerning him before Pilate, but they could prove nothing against him, and they brought false witnesses against him, and they called upon Pilate to put him to death. They crucified him that same Friday, and he suffered on Friday for six hours. These hours of our Lord's crucifixion are counted as one day. There followed three hours of darkness; these [hours] are counted as one night. Then, from the ninth hour to evening, there were three hours of day; there followed the night of *Saturday* of the passion. . . . There came the day of Saturday, and then three hours of the night after Saturday, during which Jesus slept [and rose]. Thus was fulfilled the word: The son of man must pass three days and three nights in the womb of the earth, as it is written in the Gospel. It is also written in David: Behold, thou hast disposed the days with measure. It is so written because these days and nights were shortened.[6]

Another early Christian writer, Justin Martyr, said to the Jews:

The Pasch was the Christ, as Isaiah says: Like a lamb he was led to the slaughter. It was on the day of the Pasch that you apprehended him, and it was also at the Pasch that you crucified him. . . .[7]

Furthermore, it is not until the fourth century A.D. that we find any special observance of *Holy Thursday,* although in the early days of Christianity *Holy Tuesday* was celebrated with special prayers and a Mass on the Mount of Olives. In Jerusalem itself Holy Thursday was not a special day until the beginning of the fifth century. It seems, therefore, that the early Christians treasured Holy Tuesday as the day upon which the Eucharist was instituted.

JESUS' ACTION AT THE PASSOVER

The evangelists record that at the last Passover Jesus took bread, broke it, and said, "This is my body," and took the cup saying, "This is my blood." This was not a usual practice at the Passover meal. However, there was a pre-

---

[6] Jaubert, *ibid.,* pp. 71–72, used with permission.
[7] Justin, *Dialogue* 111:3.

Christian custom in which one loaf of the Paschal unleavened bread symbolized the nation, and the piece which was broken off (the *aphikoman*) and eaten at the end of the meal symbolized the Messiah, who was broken off from his people and then restored, making the people whole.[8]

At the time of Jesus the Passover service would comprise mainly extempore prayer. Therefore, Jesus could use this custom, make it more meaningful, and identify both the bread and wine with himself.[9] Indeed, in this action Jesus may well have performed another prophetic *ôth*. Professor Daube has suggested this, and Père Dupont also has expounded on the same theme.[10] Père Dupont examines the eucharistic action within the framework of St. Mark's Gospel. He stresses that a "genuine covenant" would have been inconceivable "without a real communion in a real victim."

Mark 14 is penetrated with prophecy:[11]

1. Mark 14:3–9—the woman anointed Jesus with perfume in anticipation of his death and burial;

2. Mark 14:12–16—Jesus predicted that the disciples would meet a man with a pitcher of water and he would show them where to prepare the Passover;

3. Mark 14:18—Jesus prophesied that one of the disciples would betray him;

4. Mark 14:27 ff.—"You will all fall away; for it is written, 'I will strike the shepherd, and the sheep will be scattered'

[8] See the very important article, "He That Cometh," by David Daube, St. Paul's Lecture, published by The Council for Jewish-Christian Understanding, October 1, 1966.

[9] Apparently Professor Daube has also written upon the symbolism of the wine.

[10] J. Dupont, " 'Ceci est mon corps,' 'Ceci est mon sang,' " *Nouvelle Revue Theologique* 80 (1958), pp. 1025–1041; trans. in *Theology Digest* 9, (1961), pp. 49–51, under the title " 'This is My Body'–'This is My Blood.' "

[11] *Compare* pp. 194 f. above where we have suggested the prophetic setting of Christ's passion.

[Zech. 13:7]. But after I am raised up, I will go before you to Galilee";

5. Mark 14:30—Jesus' prediction to Peter, "Truly, I say to you, this very night, before the cock crows twice, you will deny me three times";

6. Mark 14:32–42—the Agony in the Garden where Jesus appeared clearly to foresee his passion.

Père Dupont views the institution of the Eucharist as enshrined in the midst of this prophetic activity. Dupont believes that the eucharistic gestures looked forward to the future. Jesus referred to the bread, his body, which *would* be broken, and the cup, his blood, which *would* be shed. Therefore, Jesus "broke his body unto the disciples and delivered it to them. . . . He communicated to them his blood of the Covenant. He showed them a figure of what would be done on Calvary."

In doing this Jesus behaved in a way similar, for example, to Jeremiah, who broke the potter's vessel to signify Israel's fate (Jer. 19:11).[12] To the Jewish mind this action would not be purely a sign or symbol but prophecy-in-action which "had to be efficacious." In reality, the "sacrificial rite was producing the Covenant of Calvary a day in advance."

Père Dupont's argument is convincing, but especially so if it is joined to Professor Daube's paper, mentioned previously in this chapter.[13] Jesus performed this dynamic, efficacious prophetic *ôth*, identified himself with the bread, which symbolized the Messiah, and communicated himself to the disciples.

St. Paul appears to emphasize the reality of Christ's body

---

[12] *Compare* also Acts 2:11; Ezekiel 4:1–3; 5:1–5.

[13] Professor Daube has kindly permitted the author to see the manuscript before publication.

and blood in the Eucharist and the sacrilege of receiving him unworthily in 1 Corinthians 11:27–34.[14]

THE TIMING OF THE LAST SUPPER

Père Dupont has shown the anticipation of the death of the Lord in the eucharistic gestures and the suggested chronology for Holy Week, which places the Last Supper on Tuesday night, the solar Passover, and the crucifixion on the eve of the lunar Passover. This has made the "timing" of Christ's Passion almost "too good to be true" even for divine Providence. Yet one must remember two points.

First of all, it is important to realize that the Old Testament is the revelation of God and does not pass away and fade into oblivion. It is of enduring validity and forms the foundation and only true means of understanding the New Testament. Second, it is important to understand that to the Jews contemporary with Jesus and especially to devoted men and women such as those found at Qumran, the exact date upon which a feast or salvation event occurred (or was supposed to have occurred) was of the utmost importance. In fact, one of the principal sources of contention among the different parties, for example, the Sadducees, the Pharisees, and the Essenes, was the liturgical calendar. Jesus must have understood the importance of "timing" salvation events according to the expectation of his disciples and the rest of the Jews.[15] The new redemption must take place on the day of the commemoration of the former redemption.

[14] The present writer is engaged in a study on the Hebrew background to the presence of Christ in the Eucharist.

[15] One may take as an example the tradition that the Ephraimites set out from Egypt on the wrong date and because of this error courted fatal disaster! Furthermore, one cannot overlook a certain "superstitious" dependence on astrology. Events were timed theoretically rather than historically.

Therefore, Jesus instituted the Eucharist at the Passover so that in the Jewish-Christian mind it would be intimately connected with the events commemorated at Passover, gathering up the history and theology of these and perfecting them in his own sacrificial and covenant meal. The evangelists would have understood this when they considered the life of Jesus in the light of the post-Easter faith which probably endowed them with a profound understanding of the different senses of scripture.

If we look at a synopsis of the Gospels, we can select the various elements in the Eucharist and compare them with the Old Testament sacrifices and covenants. This is not to say that the accounts in the Gospels are precise descriptions of what happened at the Last Supper but rather that they represent the matured thought of the Christian community by the time the Gospels were written down and the theological implications of the Eucharist were understood.

COVENANT ELEMENTS IN THE EUCHARIST

Matthew 26:26–29	*Mark 14:22–25*	*Luke 22:15–20*
		And he said to them, "I have earnestly desired to eat this passover with you before I suffer; for I tell you I shall not eat it until it is fulfilled in the kingdom of God."
		And he took a cup, and when he had given thanks he said, "Take this, and divide it among yourselves; for I tell you that

from now on I shall
not drink of the fruit
of the vine until the
kingdom of God
comes."

Now as they were
eating, Jesus took
bread, and blessed,
and broke it, and
gave it to the disciples
and said, "Take, eat;
this is my body."

And he took a cup,
and when he had
given thanks he gave
it to them, saying,
"Drink of it, all of
you; for this is my
blood of the cove-
nant, which is poured
out for many for the
forgiveness of sins. I
tell you I shall not
drink again of this
fruit of the vine until
that day when I drink
it new with you in my
Father's kingdom."

And as they were
eating, he took bread,
and blessed, and
broke it, and gave it
to them and said,
"Take; this is my
body."

And he took a cup,
and when he had
given thanks he gave
it to them, and they
all drank of it. And
he said to them, "This
is my blood of the
covenant, which is
poured out for many.
Truly, I say to you, I
shall not drink again
of the fruit of the
vine until that day
when I drink it new
in the kingdom of
God."

And he took bread,
and when he had
given thanks he broke
it and gave it to them,
saying, "This is my
body."

For I received from the Lord what I also delivered to you, that
the Lord Jesus on the night when he was betrayed took bread,
and when he had given thanks, he broke it, and said, "This is
my body which is broken for you. Do this in remembrance of
me." In the same way also the cup, after supper, saying, "This
cup is the new covenant in my blood. Do this, as often as you
drink it, in remembrance of me" (1 Cor. 11:23–25).

First, we see the clear reference to the death of the Lord.

Professor Jeremias[16] has shown that the phrase "flesh and blood" is a technical term denoting sacrifice; it indicates the separation of the blood (the life) from the victim. Moreover, when this is seen in conjunction with the expression "death of the Lord" (1 Cor. 11:26)—Jesus does not say my death—we recall Genesis 15: Yahweh walking through the symbols of death, the severed animals.[17] Thus, the Eucharist is the supersession of the ancient sacrifices by him who was to come and whom Abraham had seen as it were; Christ would be a pledge and reconciliation for Israel.

Second, the Eucharist is the blood of the new covenant. The Passover was not essentially a covenant meal, but it had acquired this character by its association with Genesis 15, where the promise to deliver the children of Israel from Egypt is recorded. Moreover, the blood of the new covenant fulfilled Exodus 24:6–11:

And Moses took half of the blood and put it in basins, and half of the blood he threw against the altar. Then he took the book of the covenant, and read it in the hearing of the people; and they said, "All that the Lord has spoken we will do, and we will be obedient." And Moses took the blood and threw it upon the people, and said, "Behold the blood of the covenant which the Lord has made with you in accordance with all these words."

Then Moses and Aaron, Nadab, and Abihu, and seventy of the elders of Israel went up, and they saw the God of Israel; and there was under his feet as it were a pavement of sapphire stone, like the very heaven for clearness. And he did not lay his hand

---

[16] J. Jeremias, *Eucharistic Words of Jesus,* trans. by Arnold Ehrhardt from the second German edition (Macmillan, New York, 1955), pp. 137–165, especially p. 144.

[17] See also T. H. Robinson, "My Blood of the Covenant," *Beihefte zur Zeitschrift für Die Alttestamentliche Wissenschaft* 41 (1925), pp. 232–237.

on the chief men of the people of Israel; they beheld God, and ate and drank.

The Eucharist also sealed the new Torah, which Jesus had brought to Israel.[18] It is the culmination of the exodus motif in the Gospels. In the last discourse in St. John's Gospel, in a very real way the disciples "beheld God, and ate and drank."

Third, this blood has an atoning value: ". . . this is my blood . . ., which is poured out for many for the forgiveness of sins" (Mt. 26:28; *compare* Mk. 14:24). In Jewish thought it was the blood which made atonement.

Fourth, according to the ancient covenants of pieces the parties who walked through the lane between the severed animals symbolized thereby their entering into the slaughtered victim and thence emerging in union with its life or vital essence. The parties were now identified with it, and each party shared with the others a common life. This is not a very pleasing symbolism to the modern mind, but perhaps it was a necessary preliminary to the chosen people's understanding of the new Passover as the death of Yahweh and their communion with his resurrected body.[19] Christ gives himself to Christians in the Eucharist as Yahweh gave himself and the Shekinah in the nuptial covenant on Mount Sinai.

The Eucharist perfects the covenants at which we looked in the first chapter of this book. The eucharistic meal is a contract or drawing together which establishes a special

---

[18] *Compare* also Jeremiah 31:31 and Zechariah 9:11; cf. B. W. Anderson, *op. cit.*, pp. 184. He sees an allusion to Exodus 24 in Isaiah 55:3; cf. Isaiah 54:10 and 55:1-2.

[19] See " 'Soma' as Self, Person in the Septuagint," *Neutestamentliche Studien für Rudolf Bultmann*, ed. by W. Eltester (Berlin, 1957), pp. 52–57.

relationship, a bond of communion, a common life, between two parties. So John records Jesus' words:

He who eats my flesh and drinks my blood abides in me, and I in him (Jn. 6:56).

This is a fuller realization of the knitting together of souls, as in the case of David and Jonathan (1 Sam. 18:1–4). Jesus made a covenant with his people because he loved them as his own soul, and the soul of Jesus is knit to the souls of the new chosen people.

NOTE ON THE NEW CHRONOLOGY OF HOLY WEEK

1. Sunday—Jesus entered Jerusalem and cleansed the Temple.
2. Monday—The fig tree is withered.
3. Tuesday—The Last Supper and the arrest of Jesus in the Garden took place.
4. Wednesday—A trial was held before the Jewish leaders.
5. Thursday—An early verdict trial was held by the Jews because according to Jewish law a night had to intervene before a capital sentence was imposed. Jesus was sent to Pilate. He probably spent Thursday night under the custody of Pilate. Pilate's wife experienced her dream.
6. Friday—Jesus made his last appearance before Pilate; his sentence to crucifixion was executed.

19 The Culmination of Biblical Election

The evangelists not only record that Jesus spoke of his Passion as having been foretold in Moses[1] and the prophets but also note that his resurrection from the dead on the third day was implied in scripture:

Then he said to them, "These are my words which I spoke to you, while I was still with you, that everything written about me in the law of Moses and the prophets and the psalms must be fulfilled." Then he opened their minds to understand the scriptures, and said to them, "Thus it is written, that the Christ should suffer and on the third day rise from the dead, and that repentance and forgiveness of sins should be preached in his name to all nations, begining from Jerusalem . . ." (Lk. 24:44–47).

PROPHECIES OF THE RESURRECTION

To the Pharisees asking for a sign Jesus gave only the sign of Jonah. As Jonah was in the belly of the whale for three days and three nights, so would the Son of Man be buried in the heart of the earth for three days and three nights. This was a prophecy in word, but Jesus also gave a prophecy in action. St. John records the miracle of the raising of Lazarus, and a comparison between his description

[1] That is, the Pentateuch.

218

of this event and the resurrection of Jesus shows how closely these were linked in the evangelist's mind.[2] The first seemed to drop clear hints of the second. Furthermore, Lazarus was apparently raised during the liturgical season when the lessons read concerned the deaths of the patriarchs, sickness, death, and the underworld. But there was also hope in these lessons. Among these the following text was read from Hosea 6:1–3:

> Come, let us return to the Lord;
> for he has torn, that he may heal us;
> he has stricken, and he will bind us up.
> After two days he will revive us;
> on the third day he will raise us up,
> that we may live before him.
> Let us know, let us press on to know the Lord;
> his going forth is sure as the dawn;
> he will come to us as the showers,
> as the spring rains that water the earth.

The Jews did not actually refer this text to the resurrection of the dead; rather, it was interpreted as related to the revival of the nation. The raising of Lazarus may have made the people realize that an even deeper meaning was enshrined in this text. Not only would God revive the nation, but he also would effect the resurrection of individual man and woman.[3]

---

[2] For details of this similarity between the raising of Lazarus and the resurrection of Jesus see Aileen Guilding, *The Fourth Gospel and Jewish Worship* (Oxford University Press, New York, 1960), pp. 143–153, especially p. 151.

[3] *Compare* the parable of the rich man and Lazarus. This is the only parable in which a character is given a name. At the end of the parable the rich man asks Abraham to send Lazarus to warn his five brothers about the place of torment. But Abraham said, *"They have Moses and the*

THE COVENANT MEANING OF HOSEA 6:2

> After two days he will revive us;
> on the third day he will raise us up,
> that we may live before him (Hos. 6:2).

In a recent article Dr. J. Wijngaards[4] has discussed the meaning of this text. Dr. Wijngaards rejects the interpretations which see this text in the light of the Canaanite cult and the myths of dying and rising pagan gods and goddesses. He also eliminates explanations which suggest that this text only refers to recovery from sickness. He himself proposes that this text finds its readiest interpretation when it is seen against the background of ancient vassal treaties.[5] In these treaties the dethronement of a king is described as "killing" him, even though his physical life is spared. The "killing" or dethronement is sometimes accompanied by driving him out of the land. He adds "to seek to kill a king" and "to want to have another Lord" are absolutely equivalent.

One text reads:

> Me, a dead person [   ] in the Amurru land
> on the throne of my father you have restored me. . . .
> You raised me to life.[6]

"Raising a dead vassal to life" implied that the suzerain

---

prophets; let them hear them." (Ital. mine; *compare* Lk. 24:44–47 *supra.*) It is arresting especially if, as has been suggested, the parable was told on the way to raise Lazarus.

[4] J. Wijngaards, "Death and Resurrection in Covenantal Context (Hos. VI 2)," *Vetus Testamentum* 17 (April 1967), pp. 226–239. Quotations used with permission of E. J. Brill, Leiden.

[5] *Compare* pp. 61 ff. above.

[6] Wijngaards, *op. cit.*, 233.

reinstated him as ruler of the country and granted him the full blessing of life and fertility, which he could communicate to his subjects. Dr. Wijngaards suggests that it is against this background that we should understand Hosea 6:1–3. "In the light of this ancient, international covenant terminology" the Prophet Hosea expressed the hope that even after his people's defection[7] Yahweh would "revive them again" by renewing the covenant. Covenant terminology is found in the words "to return," which denote reconciliation with Yahweh: "Let us know Yahweh" is a parallel expression. The phrases "after two days" and "on the third day" (Hos. 6:2) may derive from the covenantal custom of celebrating the pact "in the morning on the third day" (*compare* Amos 4:4–13).

Thus, the resurrection mentioned in this passage of Hosea can be interpreted as covenantal language.

In Hosea 6:3 Jahweh is said to "revive" and "raise" his people when "on the third day" he will renew his covenant with them. This renewal is called a "raising from death to life" because it will restore the reign of blessing and fertility that are consequent on and inherent in good covenantal relations.[8]

Dr. Wijngaards concludes his article by commenting briefly on the importance of recognizing the covenantal terminology, which was still known and practiced in Christ's day, in order to understand Christ's death and resurrection as the implementation of the new covenant. He adds that it is not a small wonder "that Christ's rising on the third

---

[7] In Hosea 13:1 Israel is said to have died because of their sin with Baal. Yahweh is described as killing Israel (Hos. 2:3; 9:5) or redeeming them from death (Hos. 12:14) (ibid. p. 238). This idea of dying through sin is used frequently in the New Testament.

[8] Wijngaards, *op. cit.,* 237.

day" was considered of paramount importance (mentioned 18 times in the New Testament): apart from it being the natural day on which to conclude the covenant, it was in harmony with the prophecy of Hosea 6:1–3 which held out the promise of the messianic revival "on the third day!" In spite of the absence of explicit references to Hosea 6:1–3 in the New Testament, we may well presuppose this prophecy wherever it mentions Christ's resurrection on the third day. And it *may* be that the apostolic witnesses *did* have Hosea 6:2 in mind when they claimed that the resurrection happened "in accordance with the scriptures" (1 Cor. 15:4; cf. Lk. 24:46).

THE COVENANT AND THE RESURRECTION

If this theory is correct, one sees the hope of resurrection running through the traditions (biblical and extra-biblical) concerning the covenant of God with his people. Genesis 15 promised a type of "resurrection" in the posterity promised to an old man and an old woman considered dead by contemporary society because of their childlessness (*compare* Rom. 4:19).[9] The same text also promised a "resurrection" from slavery to the chosen descendants of this elect man and this elect woman. The extra-biblical texts chose to see the undivided birds of Genesis 15 as symbols of the resurrection of the dead. Extra-biblical texts also injected the hope of resurrection into the story of the Binding of Isaac.

The Exodus event saw the rebirth of a nation by its formal covenant with King Yahweh. To defect from that covenant was "death"; to be incorporated into it meant "life." Toward the preservation of that life all the prophets devoted their lives.

[9] *Compare* Genesis 30:1–2.

It remained for the Son of God himself to become flesh, to incorporate into himself all Israel, and to be the personification of that covenant. He was "driven out of the land," because his suzerainty was rejected. He was killed in body, but he rose on the third day and thereby created the covenant anew. Thus, throughout the biblical text the idea of resurrection gradually becomes clearer and more concrete until it culminates in the bodily resurrection of the Son of God.

Jesus' resurrection was preceded by his passion, a suffering which was not unproductive; as the pains of childbirth bring forth a new life, it brought forth a new community. This community under the patronage of the new "Abraham"[10] was to become a mission community to the nations, and thus Matthew 28:18–19 fulfilled Genesis 12:1–3.

Matthew 28:18–19	*Genesis 12:1–3*
And Jesus came and said to them, "All authority in heaven and on earth has been given to me. Go therefore and make disciples of all nations, baptizing them in the name of the Father and of the Son and of the Holy Spirit."	Now the Lord said to Abram, "Go from your country and your kindred and your father's house to the land that I will show you. And I will make of you a great nation, and I will bless you, and make your name great, so that you will be a blessing. I will bless those who bless you, and him who curses you I will curse; and by you all the families of the earth shall bless themselves."

This mission community was fully created when Christ ascended to the right hand of God and, having reestablished his kingship and priesthood, poured forth the gift of the

10 *Compare* pp. 184 ff. above.

Holy Spirit upon those who believed in him.[11] Thus, the Shekinah descended once more to dwell among the chosen people in the Body of Christ, the Church. The Church became the Bride of Christ as Israel was the Bride of Yahweh, and in this way the earthly family of Abraham was caught up into the heavenly.[12] Perhaps few people have expressed this so vividly as Melito of Sardis, a second-century bishop, who delivered an Easter homily showing how Christ's passion and resurrection fulfilled Moses and the Prophets. He concludes,

. . . but he arose from the [dead to the heights of the] heavens, God who put on man, and suffered for the sufferer, and was bound for him who was bound and judged for him who was condemned, and buried for him who was buried.

[And he] arose from the dead and cries thus [to you]: "Who is he that contendeth against me? Let him stand before me. I freed the condemned, I made the dead to live again, I raise him who was buried. Who is he who raises his voice against me? I," he says, "am the Christ, I am he who put down death, and triumphed over the enemy, and trod upon Hades, and bound the strong one and brought man safely home to the heights of the heavens; I," he says, "Christ."

"Therefore, come hither all ye families of men, who are sullied with sins, and receive remission of sins. For I am your remission. I am the Passover of salvation, the Lamb that was sacrificed for you, I am your ransom [?], I am your light, I am your savior, I am the resurrection, I am your king, I lead you up to the heights of the heavens, I will show you the Father who is from the ages, I will raise you up by my right hand."

[11] *Compare* Ephesians 4:1–16.
[12] *Compare* Revelation 21:1–4

This is he who first made heaven and earth, who in the beginning [created] man, who was proclaimed by Law and Prophets, who was buried in the earth, who [rose] from the dead and went up to [the heights of heaven] and sitteth at the right hand of the Father.[13]

FURTHER READING

Charles, R. H., *Eschatology: The Doctrine of a Future Life in Israel, Judaism and Christianity*. Schocken, New York, 1963.

Durrwell, F. X., *The Resurrection. A Biblical Study*, trans. by Rosemary Sheed. Sheed and Ward, New York, 1960.

Ramsey, A. M., *The Resurrection of Christ*, 2nd ed. Allenson, Naperville, Ill., 1956.

Stanley, D. M., *Christ's Resurrection in Pauline Soteriology*. Pontifical Biblical Institute, Rome, 1961.

[13] *The Homily on the Passion by Melito of Sardis with some Fragments of the Apocryphal Ezekiel*, trans. by Campbell Bonner in *Studies and Documents*, ed. by K. Lake and S. Lake, 12 (University of Pennsylvania Press, Philadelphia, 1940), used with permission.

Index of Principal Scriptural Citations

Index of Principal Biblical Names

Index of Principal
Non-Biblical Names

233

Index of Principal Subjects

235